G000146356

PAUL & ANNIE'S GREAT BIG TANDEM TOUR!

Annie Roebuck

Onwards and Upwards Publishers

Berkeley House
11 Nightingale Crescent
Leatherhead
Surrey
KT24 6PD

www.onwardsandupwards.org

Printed in the UK by 4edge Limited.

ISBN: 978-1-911086-06-2
Typeface: Calibri / KBScaredStraight

For Sheila, Sara, and Jonny;

your laughter, wisdom, humour and
positivity are treasures in my life.

Contents

Foreword 7

How it All Began 9

Land's End to Ponsonooth 25

Ponsonooth to Callington 40

Callington to Exeter 50

Exeter to Pawlett 60

Pawlett to Thornbury 69

Thornbury to Evesham 79

Evesham to Rugby 90

Rugby to Barton-under-Needwood 98

Barton-under-Needwood to Bosley 108

Bosley to Rainford 119

Rainford to Carnforth 128

Carnforth to Langwathy 139

Langwathy to Eskdalemuir 149

Eskdalemuir to Penicuik 161

Penicuik to Perth 174

Perth to Calvine 187

Calvine to Carrbridge 197

Carrbridge to Allness 207

Allness to Helmsdale 218

Helmsdale to John O' Groats 228

Foreword

When Annie first dropped the bombshell on us, we had to admit to experiencing slight – or perhaps that should read *great* – feelings of apprehension.

Annie ride tandem with husband Paul from Land's End to John O' Groats?

We have known Annie and Paul for twenty-five years and worked with them both at the Macclesfield Christian Mission; Paul as our much valued Mission treasurer, and Annie as the paid youth evangelist. We had vivid memories of her aversion to physical exercise (she frequently complained about climbing the stairs to the Mission office). Then there was her need of an alarming amount of chocolate to maintain her energy levels; and, more seriously, what about the problem with her back?

We found it hard to envisage her completing such a huge challenge!

The fact that Paul was a super fit cyclist allayed our fears somewhat. Would it finish up with Paul on the front of the tandem doing all the pedalling while Annie gazed at the countryside as they sped through? It was true that Annie would occupy the back seat, but she swiftly disillusioned us about the idea of her not pedalling: "That doesn't work on a tandem," she informed us, having obviously heard this particular remark many times before.

We felt some concern for the unsuspecting hosts they'd coerced into offering generous hospitality along the way; would they survive intact?

All our fears proved totally unfounded. Annie trained hard; Paul worked out the route with his usual efficiency and ensured the tandem was kept in full working order.

Having selected two very worthwhile charities they wanted to support with the sponsorship money they raised, they intended to succeed no matter what.

So, congratulations, Annie & Paul, on completing the trip. Especial congratulations to Annie too, on keeping up the humour-filled blog so faithfully, on bad days as well as good, as their journey proceeded northwards. Fortunately, she can always see the funny side of bizarre events – though sometimes not till some while after they happen.

If you enjoy a good read of a true story that may occasionally make you groan in sympathy but provides a smile on every page, that will make you chuckle frequently and often laugh out loud – turn the page and read on...

Stuart & Janet George
Retired Directors of Macclesfield Christian Mission

How it All Began

Single bikes were never going to work for us. Paul is a keen cyclist; cycling is to him what breathing is to most people, but I am neither a cyclist nor keen. He was probably born clutching a bike pump tightly in his fist and he has the legs, the stamina and the mindset for going out on two wheels whereas I am more of a coffee shop kind of girl with the physique to match. Even with that nugget of information in his head, it didn't stop him from buying me a pretty pink and green bike shortly after we were married in '94; such are the dreams of young love! The bike decorated our garage for the next ten years and probably went out the same number of times.

I grew into the habit of re-naming hills that we rode. For example, there's one near us just the other side of Congleton that I call Brussels Sprout Hill, the reason being this: you fly down one side of a valley to a beautiful bridge over the river Dane only to have to climb up out again the other side, and whichever way you approach it that's how it's going to play out; a bit like eating a good roast dinner, you still have the Brussels sprouts at the end. So when on one memorable bike ride I renamed a lane with an incline Divorce Hill, I think Paul got the message that I was not happy.

Friends suggested we borrow their tandem and that's where it all started. We used their tandem for a couple of years – it was a Dawes, I think – and then bought a second-hand one from a chap in Buxton – that was an Orbit. The problem with single bikes is that I could never keep up with Paul, and he nearly fell off his bike going so slow waiting for me as I huffed and puffed my way round Cheshire. You don't have that problem on a tandem obviously! We discovered riding together was actually quite fun, and went further afield on our adventures. In those days it was a map and compass job but it worked; it satisfied Paul's desire to share his love of cycling with me and it satisfied my desire to spend time with him; it was a win-win.

In 2007 we decided to embark on a tour of friends and relatives around the midlands and thought the Orbit was an accident waiting to happen, so we ditched it (giving it to my sister!) and invested in a brand new mid-range priced red tandem by Landescape. Whilst Paul dealt with all the specifications and finances, I wandered round the shop and picked up a book: 'Land's End to John O' Groats – The Great British Bike Adventure' by Phil Horsley. It proved an entertaining read and I commented to Paul,

"We should do this one day!"

After all, I didn't find reading the book exhausting at all. It was a throwaway line but it lodged in Paul's head and most likely his heart too, though he knows I often have spontaneous ideas that are not always rooted in reality; like the time I nearly bought him a Vietnamese pot-bellied pig for his birthday simply because he likes the creatures. I said we could keep it in the garden.

He vetoed that one.

Then there was the time I bought twenty-two rainbow trout from a door-to-door salesman because I thought it was a good idea at the time. Three years later we needed the freezer space and threw them away.

The midland tour was a success; we prepared by doing training runs on the Isle of Wight, a place we love dearly. Anyone who has cycled on the island will know how good the training was as there are hills at every turn. The run along the 'back o' the Wight' from Blackgang to Freshwater Bay, cycling the length of Military Road, remained my favourite route for years until we headed up the Drummochter pass in Scotland, and now they share the prize. The training wasn't easy; my dad had just died and I was to speak at his funeral, so each day as we went out I prepared in my head what I would say. To be fair, it gave me something to concentrate on as we slogged up the hills. Whenever we cycle particular routes on the island now my thoughts go straight back to that time, and to him.

The first leg of our midland tour was from Macclesfield to Shrewsbury to stay with my mother. From there we went to Hereford, Evesham, Birmingham, back to Shrewsbury and then back to Macclesfield. At one point ten miles out from Shrewsbury I got off the tandem and declared I was never getting back on it. I like to set Paul these little challenges. He had to coax me back on the saddle and then persuade me to stay on it to Shrewsbury and then home. In all, we did just over three hundred miles that week. It had been a huge challenge for us both but not one that I was willing to repeat.

Fast forward six years to August 2013. My nephew Matt and his lovely wife Anna decided to do Land's End to John O' Groats (henceforth referred to as LEJOG) that summer, and stayed with us at our lodge in Bosley, Cheshire on day five of their journey. They were on single bikes and we were in awe of them. We fed them, bathed them, massaged their aches and pains and listened to their tale; it was so inspirational that I suddenly heard my voice say,

"We have to do this, Paul!" That's twice now!

After all, I had read the book. What other training did I need! Paul wasn't so convinced and, unusually for him, was more reluctant to 'seize the day'. His heart was singing but his head was saying, "Who are you and what have you done with my wife?"

"We go out on the tandem every week between now and Christmas and you lose some weight, and then I'll know you're serious," he challenged me.

To be fair, I was fourteen stone at the time and maybe the idea of dragging all that weight behind him up the country didn't appeal so much; plus the fact that we only ever went out on the tandem on high days and holidays suggests he was probably right to be a little cautious.

Like a woman possessed, I threw myself into a regime of cycling, keep fit, and interval training, and lost all of one stone by Christmas, but that was enough to convince Paul I was serious and so we set the date. 15th May, 2014 was going to be Day One of *Paul and Annie's Great Big Tandem Tour!*

Paul had to arrange for time off work. Fortunately, he works at a school with all the holidays included, and as he is semi-retired –

he's sixty-one, you know! – that meant as a part-timer they allowed him to shift his hours around.

"How many miles would you like to do each day?" Paul asked. I was tempted to say ten, but with a thousand miles ahead of us that would take wa-a-a-ay too long, even with his school's gracious backing, so I opted for fifty. That would still be twenty days of cycling. I wasn't working at the time so three weeks was doable with Paul's half term taken into account.

I remembered a piece of good advice I had read in 'that' book years before, which went along the lines of, "Make sure you can get to and from your starting point and destination before you work out your route." This proved harder than one would imagine. Trains go to Penzance but not all take bikes and even less take tandems; the same goes for Thurso near John O' Groats. We then thought of hiring a van to get us there and another to get us back, but that was very costly.

I phoned my sister Shirley and told her how our plans were not going well.

"Drive to us in Exeter with the tandem on your bike carrier, insure me on your car and I'll take you to Land's End, drop you off, and pick you up in Scotland three weeks later."

I am very blessed with a practical thinking, straightforward, encouraging sister who would go to the ends of the world – well, Britain anyway – to help us out. If only the rest of the tour were that easy!

(I really should tell her to scrap the bike we gave her.)

Shirley also suggested that as I was a Methodist local preacher, I should phone all churches in the areas we were hoping to stay in and see if anyone could put us up for the night. We had decided to do the tour on behalf of two charities, one of them being 'The Methodist Relief and Development Fund'[1], so that's what we did. Paul's job was to map out the route, and mine was to contact churches along the way. We had learned from Matt and Anna's experience of not knowing the route thoroughly and were not going to go down the same road (no pun intended) and so it was that Paul spent many hours on the computer working out our daily routes in fine detail right down to the last bush – believe me, he went on Google Earth to see what the roads looked like! – and then transferring it to the GPS for the bike. I made phone calls around the country and had conversations with people I had never met, explaining the tour and cheekily asking them if someone in their fellowship might be kind enough to put us up for the night. All bar one said yes.

By the turn of the New Year, we started to consciously involve God in all our planning, and prayed most nights about the tour. Paul prayed for practical wisdom, places to stay, organising the route etc.; I prayed that we wouldn't get squashed under a lorry. Only as the tour unfolded did I begin to realise that actually God had orchestrated the whole thing, and we were part of his plans rather than he part of ours.

The next step was to gain support for ourselves and the charities; the other one being 'Christian Relief Uganda', a charity close to our hearts with Paul serving as a member on the executive

---

[1] Now called 'All We Can'.

board. As a Methodist preacher, I usually prepare a new sermon each time I preach within the circuit. This year I armed myself with one – 'Things I have learned about God on the back of the Tandem – trust, balance, perseverance' – and took it to all the churches I was designated to preach at from January onwards, along with the tandem and Paul as visual aids.

Paul and I are not particularly publicity-minded and after having bemoaned that fact between us one day at Costa Coffee in town, imagine our surprise when the very next day a friend at church offered to take on the promotional side of the tour. Jason became our media mogul and, with his vision and energy for stuff like this, was a literal answer to prayer! He designed the flyers advertising the tour and we had 2500 printed. When they arrived, I did have a little cry. "Good grief!" I thought. It was now a reality; no longer could I live in La La Land, this really was happening; there it was in multi-coloured print. I wanted to do it... and I didn't want to do it. It was an odd place to be at in my head. But for the moment, in the main, I was caught up in all the preparation and excitement that it engendered.

We distributed the flyers far and wide in churches, coffee shops, to friends, family, local tourist information centres, schools, *anywhere* just to get rid of the huge pile. We sent them ahead of us to the people we would be staying with on the tour so that they had a picture of what we hoped to look like when we turned up at their door. As it turned out, we never did look like the pristine couple on the flyer – we always looked sweaty, exhausted, wet, harassed and bedraggled – but they seemed to recognise us.

Jason wrote an article for the local newspaper, and suggested that we should write a blog whilst on the tour. My head began to spin. I felt everything was getting far too complicated, and as I am technophobic to boot, I was not at all keen to take that particular idea on board; it was one step too far. Jason had other ideas though and before I could say, "Can't we use pigeons instead?" he had the blog site up and running and encouraged me to write a weekly report from February onwards with news of our preparations. We had five faithful followers to begin with: my sister; my mother; our two sons, Jamie and Simon; and David, a friend from church. Since I spoke to each of them regularly anyway, I couldn't see the point, but Jason insisted and I didn't want to upset him, so I persevered.

We took the bike to Yorkshire for its M.O.T. at J. D. Tandems in Gargrave, where it had been born, and whilst there decided to get some training in. Around Ingleton there are hills in every direction and we also discovered the best little coffee shop in Kirkby Lonsdale for lattes and cake; so 'training' went well from my perspective. We were going out on the tandem two to three times a week and covering about thirty miles each time. This was a far cry from the fifty miles a day for twenty days straight we would have to do on the tour and I started to fret that I wouldn't be able to complete the challenge and would let everyone down.

Paul cuddled me and said, "You can do this. I know you can."

My personal trainer at the fitness club said the same thing, but he didn't cuddle me.

Sometimes, when we can't see the wood for the trees, it's good to have someone who can help steer you through the rough bits.

It's good to talk.

Around the end of March, I applied for a job vacancy as a Family Outreach Worker in my home church. One of the interviewers was an admirable lady called Avril.

"I hear you are doing Land's End to John O' Groats soon. I did it myself, a while back," she said.

"O, hey, that's great! How long did it take you?"

"Five days. How long are you giving yourself to complete it?"

"Three weeks," I whispered.

Ha-ha! We did laugh. Five days works out around two hundred miles a day, and I remember saying that even if I didn't get the job, it had been worth coming to the interview just to be inspired not to complain about fifty miles ever again.

I got the job (not for that comment, I hasten to add… I hope…) This was a good thing but added more pressure into the mix, and I had the added hassle of sorting out 'holiday' from work barely three weeks after I started, at the beginning of May – but my church minister, Derek, was sympathetic and gave me a special dispensation.

Paul was as happy as a sandboy in all of this. Due to painful circumstances, we had left our previous church three years earlier and Paul was still in a place of grieving, so this adventure took him out of himself and he enjoyed all the planning and training. He had an app on his GPS that showed the profile of the journey; it looked like a very bad heart trace on an ECG machine. What on earth had I gotten myself into? As the time drew nearer, he was like a coiled up spring; he was desperate to do it there and then.

I was happy to wait.

Whenever we talked about the tour (which was all the time by now), Paul was all about the cycling and I was all about the food we would eat en route – hey, it's the way God made me!

I wondered if we'd eat real haggis in Scotland.

Three weeks before our start date, Paul went down with flu – not man flu either, this was the real deal. Paul is rarely ill and never a good patient so it was hard work all round, but better now than in three weeks' time. On our final training ride we went to the coffee shop at Astbury Garden Centre (my second home) and by chance got chatting with a cyclist from Chester who had done LEJOG in 2009. He was able to give us some useful insights and tips – like, "Don't do it!" – whilst we all sat round eating cake. By the end of our conversation, I was officially terrified. On the way home we invested in expensive lightweight, waterproof, windproof, sweat-proof jackets, and plenty of special cream for our delicate bottoms.

One day we packed the panniers full just to see how much our luggage would weigh, and had to promptly re-think the whole thing. I volunteered to stay at home to lighten the load but Paul was hearing none of it (partly because he had since gone almost deaf in his left ear following an infection after the flu). We decided to travel as light at possible, even to the extent of sharing a toothbrush; some teenagers I spoke to were horrified at this revelation.

"It's what you do when you're married and desperate," I said.

I think I successfully put them off walking down the aisle for a fair few years.

Even so, our panniers together with the top box full of bike tools, spare inner tubes, folding tyre etc. weighed two stone.

In our last Sunday service at church before the tour began we were given a jolly good send-off; everyone was buzzing with excitement except possibly me who still thought we would end up under a truck. It was all a bit surreal, to be honest. I set up a huge map of Britain at church with the route marked on it, and provided a big moveable fluorescent arrow – "we are here" – so that the fellowship could follow our adventure. Our minister Derek prayed for us and then we all sang a song that he had rewritten with us in mind.

If you know 'One More Step Along The World I Go', then sing along to the slightly new version. Enjoy!

Paul and Annie on their tandem tour,
Tip of Cornwall to the Northern shore,
From one county to the new,
Keep them travelling along with you.

God the Son, the Father, and the Spirit too,
Bless them as they tandem on with you!

As they travel through the bad and good,
Keep them pedalling the way they should.
May they find the way to go,
Knowing always that you love them so.

Give them courage when the road is rough,
Keep them loving when the going is tough.
Energy in all they do,
Keep them travelling along with you.

Give them friendships all along the way,
Comfy beds for every night-time's stay.
Food and drink and lots of tea,
Puncture, accident and illness free!

On 14th May, 2014 we set off for Exeter just after 1pm, after I had nipped to Key Green Church coffee morning to do a last minute plug. Our son Simon and daughter-in-law Charlotte came to wave us off. I was very emotional at this point but did cheer up hugely after a hilarious conversation with them both. I commented that this escapade would be like a second honeymoon, being with Paul every day for three weeks. Charlotte misunderstood and was mortified that her in-laws might engage in anything else but sleep whilst staying in someone else's home.

"You can't do that sort of thing; it's just not right."

And I thought the young were liberated!

As it turned out, we were just too tired to indulge in 'that sort of thing' whilst on the tour, but I couldn't resist teasing Charlotte, and every so often I would send her the text,

"...another night, another guest bed!..."

We mounted the tandem on the car roof tandem carrier, which involves putting the front wheel in the boot, otherwise the bike overhangs too far.

Charlotte came out and said, "You do realise there's a wheel missing?"

Sometimes I worry about her.

The M6 was a car park but we eventually arrived in Exeter around 6.30pm. We were watered, fed and walked by my sister

and brother-in-law Malcolm, and went to bed early to dream sweet dreams of… beaches, gardens, coffee shops… anything but cycling!

We slept in their bed that night so I did warn them of what might occur, however it's so huge that Paul needed his GPS just to find me.

Comments / Texts

Remember, guest beds however big or small are just for sleeping in and nothing else!

Simon

Bon voyage, as you set off on your expedition… don't hesitate to call for help if you need it when you get to the Midlands, happy to help if poss.

Jamie

I will need help in the Midlands, I will need you to SIT ON THE BACK OF THE BIKE.

Annie

Annie, fear not! If your pedalling is as good as your preaching, I foresee a cake and chocolate famine in John O' Groats!

David and Pam

Wishing you every success as you begin your journey! The chronicle is running a piece on you and want to know your ages, is that OK?

Jason

Paul is 61, I'm a very youthful 52.

Annie

Wishing you both all the very best on your epic journey, I'll be following every pedal of the way. Love you both lots, take extra special care xxx

Pat

Thank you. I've shown Charlotte where your birthday pressie is just in case we get splattered!

Annie

Hoping everything's going well with your final arrangements, and that you have an absolutely fantastic time on the tour. We'll be thinking and praying for you both, lots of love and God bless!

Geoff and Claire

Excited, nervous… this is our second honeymoon after all!

Annie

Can't believe you're sharing a toothbrush!! Yuck!! You've obviously been married longer than us!!!

Simon

My thoughts too, Simon… told Jamie there was no chance!!!

Pam

All the best on your journey. I'm sure you'll learn and experience lots. You'll make many new friends and probably some lifelong ones. There'll be ups and downs (I pray for less downs) but most importantly I pray you grow closer to God as you ride through his beautiful landscape and that you raise lots of money for great causes. All the very best. The MacGregor clan

xxx

BON VOYAGE, OUR WONDERFUL FRIENDS! We will be praying and blogging you every day and all the way. Lots of love, Ian and Jude

Jude

May the road rise up to meet you.
May the wind be always at your back.
May the sun shine warm upon your face;
the rains fall soft upon your fields
and until we meet again,
may God hold you in the palm of His hand.

Looking forward to seeing you near Inverness

David and Rachel

15TH MAY, 2014

STAGE 1

Land's End to Ponsonooth

Every journey starts with a single turn of the pedal.

We began our journey from Exeter to Land's end around 9am. Before we left, I spent a good part of half an hour perched on the toilet and later discovered that this was to become my way of life for the next twenty days; it must be something to do with nerves.

We decided to start the tour in style so I wore Chanel courtesy of my sister Shirley, and Paul wore Givenchy courtesy of Malcolm. In our desire to travel light we carried no such luxuries with us, though I did pack three small perfumes from Avon – Today, Tomorrow and Forever – and wore them according to my mood. On a good flat day it was Today because I knew it would be enjoyable; on a hilly day it was Tomorrow because I would need something to look forward to, and on days that I was dreading it would be Forever because that's how long I suspected they would go on for.

Paul moved the bike carrier from our car to my sister's – hers is bigger and more roomy for travelling – and after waving goodbye to my mother who was by now living in Exeter too, we set off with Shirley and Malcolm to face our destiny. It was an interesting journey down the A30. We saw Dartmoor from a distance, and that was bad enough; we were going to have to climb it in two days' time. (That would be a Forever day, clearly.) Malcolm decided to get creative and took photos of the tandem's shadow on the road as we bombed along at 60mph; the pictures looked quite good actually. Someone commented that the tandem wasn't going to go at that speed for the next three weeks and everyone laughed – except me, who felt just ever so slightly, definitely sick. By the time we got to Land's End, I was a bag of nerves. I'd held Paul's hand in the car on the journey and kept looking at him in a way that says,

"We're doomed, doomed!"

Paul kept remarking he was jolly glad this had been my idea or I would be hitting him by now.

Yes, it *was* my idea but he could have said no, and for that and the fact that he kept saying, "It was your idea," I still felt like hitting him.

We arrived at Land's End car park to be met by the parking attendant who cheerfully asked for a £5 fee. He then noticed the tandem on the roof rack – how could he not? – and said,

"Where are you heading?"

I felt like saying, "The grave," but out of the blue a rush of bravado and demand for respect took me over and I said, "John O' Groats," with as much fortitude as I could muster. Apparently these are magic words and the fee was wavered (so it's worth it for something then).

My ever thoughtful sister had packed a flask of tea and as the men took the tandem off the roof rack and assembled all relevant parts, Shirley and I walked over to the rocks near the sea where I experienced a sudden unnerving desire to throw myself in – but had a cup of tea instead. People who know me understand just how important a little thing like a cup of tea is to me so I was thankful that Shirley had had the foresight to think of it. She had packed some food too but the knot in my stomach would only let liquids through.

We walked through the shopping square to the marker post that boasts "Land's End" at the top of it, and points to John O' Groats, 874 miles north. Now, I am no mathematician but even I know that 874 is not the same number as 980, which is how many miles Paul told me we were going to cycle, so I immediately had a bit of a paddy demanding to know where these extra 106 miles had appeared from. Paul explained that as we were staying in Rugby and later on at our home in Bosley, plus all the extra little roads to get to our hosts each night, the route we were taking was "inevitably longer".

We ended up cycling 1018 miles by the end of the tour; 144 miles "inevitably longer"...

Shirley prayed the 'priestly blessing' from chapter 6 of the book of Numbers in the Bible over us as she and Malcolm gathered us close.

"The Lord bless you and keep you; the Lord make his face shine upon you and be gracious to you; the Lord turn his face towards you and give you peace."

I have prayed these words over each of my grandchildren when I held them for the first time at the start of their own incredible journey through life, so these words seemed fitting for this occasion.

Hugs were heartfelt, photos were taken, smiles were nervous – and suddenly we were off! As we cycled back up through the square I waved furiously at my sister:

"I love you, I love you. See you at John O' Groats!" I shouted, and then started waving at everyone around us too; it felt like a party atmosphere such was the adrenaline rush.

"She's not a shy girl, is she?" Shirley commented to Malcolm.

Once we were actually on the tandem and the tour had officially begun, I became a different person; we were both buzzed up with excitement and chatted and laughed and enjoyed the scenery. This was it; all the planning, the phone calls, the preparation was behind us; before us lay the length of Britain.

We were on a mission, we were adventurers, we were inspired, we were steaming, we rocketed along.

We stopped.

After just four miles we hit Trethaway, and although we made it up the first part of the hill, when we got to the hairpin bend with a nasty camber we had no choice but to get off as we were almost cycling backwards. This did nothing to dampen our spirits though and after walking fifty feet we got back on the saddle and were off once more.

We rode through Newlyn on our way to Penzance which would have been a wonderful downhill, wind-in-your-face experience, had it not been for a truckload of grass in front of us that crawled along at the pace of a snail, and the only thing I got in my face was grass as it danced through the air. I loathe the smell of cut grass, I can't breathe properly. Hay fever. Yay!

We reached a top speed of 39.2mph later in the day which made up for the slow pace at this point.

We had cycled all of twelve miles when we got to Penzance and decided to stop for lunch; it was about 1pm by now and we both needed food. We found the open Lido and sat beside it eating our jam sandwiches, when my mobile buzzed.

Before the tour I had invested in a Bluetooth earpiece for such a time as this. We have made many good friends at our home church, Wellspring, and in our house-group in particular. Two friends there, Ian and Derek, are truckers and occasionally phone me during the week to continue some theological discussion; usually when they are stuck on the M6 with nothing better to do, and they think, "I'll phone Annie."

I'm glad I have my uses.

Anyhow, Derek had suggested I get this Bluetooth device so that we could chat during the days of cycling without me having to stop and pull my phone out. Derek and Ian's daily log-ins became part and parcel of the tour, and they were my encouragers, coaches, confidants and pick-me-ups, and many of the conversations were full of laughter. I am eternally grateful to them and the M6 for that.

Paul is grateful too; whenever either of them phoned, I got so wrapped up in conversation I didn't notice the hills quite so much or my very painful derrière, and it meant he could put a wriggle on and I wouldn't complain. Ian always managed to phone when we were having a coffee stop, or going on the flat; whenever Derek phoned we were heading uphill, or exhausted near the end of the day.

It was Ian who phoned now. He knew the Lido where we were sitting but it had been so damaged by storms and excessive rain earlier in the year that it was just a shadow of its former glory and certainly not something I would choose to bathe in. Even so, the weather was beautiful, Penzance was beautiful, the sea was beautiful, and I felt pretty good too; and we were off again cycling along the seafront towards Marazion and St Michael's Mount. I guess it would have been pleasant to stride across the causeway but we were too psyched up to stop and take a detour. How many times I got off the tandem though to take "just one more picture" is anyone's guess; I deleted most of them in the end.

From there on it seemed we cycled the next twenty miles up every hill Paul could possibly find in the vicinity of our night's resting place at Ponsonooth. All I can say is, it's a good job he had me on the back of the bike to help push and pedal.

We only did thirty-four miles that first day, having wanted to split the journey through Cornwall over three days. We cycled through Trescowe, Godolphin Cross, Nancegollan, Porkellis, Rame and Stithians, all of them 'up' and all with a funny noise emanating from the rear end of the bike. Perhaps the tandem had a soul after all and was complaining with me about the hills, or maybe it was just complaining *about* me – I'm not sure – but four miles out from Ponsanooth we had to get off and take a good look.

We discovered that the bolt holding the pannier rack on the right hand side had sheared off completely. I felt this was entirely due to the fact that I had given in to my son's pleas to take my own toothbrush; it was without a doubt the last straw that broke the camel's back, or the carrier's bolt in this case.

Paul knew it would need a temporary mend at least and set about fixing it. He had had the foresight to pack some cable ties "just in case" and needed to locate them somewhere near the bottom of one of the panniers. He unpacked various articles to make them easier to reach and never did I imagine that I would see my nightie and knickers lying unceremoniously at the side of the road, but there they were. I thought of all the bugs that would be crawling in and out, or maybe just crawling in; and started feeling an itch here, and a leg or two there. *Urggh!*

Derek phoned twice in those last few miles but the signal was rubbish so all I heard was,

"Hi, it's Dere..." and

"Hi, it's m..."

But I appreciated the effort.

We arrived shortly after 4pm at the home of Chris and Estelle. I was clearly delirious at this point because when the woman of the house answered the door I said,

"Hello, are you Chris?" Did I really think her husband would be called Estelle?

With a warm welcome and a drink inside us – "Tea, please, weak, milky, no sugar; and coffee, white with one, thanks" became our mantra over the next three weeks – we were ready for a shower. Chris and Estelle's home is upside down; I don't mean it's a bomb site by that, I mean that the bedrooms are downstairs and the living space and kitchen up. They had been flooded out five months previously during the terrible storms that hit the south coast and used our arrival date as the deadline to get things done. Well, it looked designer-lush now, and our bedroom looking out to the back garden was a haven of rest.

We began a routine that day that we stuck to ever after like glue:

- Arrival.
- Tidings.
- Bike safely stored in garage.
- Me drink and chat to hosts; Paul shower.
- Paul drink and chat to hosts; me bath (where possible).
- Text small group of friends (henceforth called 'the super seven') re. safe arrival.
- Write blog. Choose photos to accompany it. Send blog.
- Eat.
- Conversation.

- Early to bed.
- Write diary.
- Pray.
- Sleep.

We had it down to a fine art within the first few days; it was the only way we could function.

We quickly developed a morning routine as well:

- Paul up at 7 to shave, wash and dress.
- Me up at 7.30 to shave, wash and dress. (Just joking. I don't shave; I pluck.)
- Breakfast at 8am.
- Me on toilet from about 8.30 whilst Paul re-packed the panniers.
- Check route.
- Pray.
- Leave around 9am.

Estelle cooked a meal of chicken casserole, followed by apple crumble with real Cornish cream. I love my food and thank God every day for my taste buds.

We enjoyed a wonderful evening with our hosts and their son Ben as they shared with us their God-given vision for their church's new community building. It was at a crucial stage at this point with problems arising concerning the building regs, and yet they still had time to look after us.

Chris had a phone call on the matter and Paul took the opportunity to give the bike a once over, securing the pannier rack with more cable ties and insulation tape. By the time he had finished, nothing was ever going to move anywhere ever again.

Estelle and I chatted and I shared with her a poem I had in my keeping called 'The Road of Life'. I read it several times over the course of the tour and found it quite insightful; it sums up so much about my relationship with God and is reinforced by my experiences on the back of the tandem.

I'm sure you will understand why as you read it now.

At first I saw God as my observer, my judge,
keeping track of the things I did wrong,
so as to know whether I merited heaven or hell when I die.
He was out there sort of like a president;
I recognized His picture when I saw it,
but I didn't really know Him.

But later on
when I met Christ,
it seemed as though life were rather like a bike ride,
but it was a tandem bike,
and I noticed that Christ
was in the back helping me pedal.

I don't know just when it was
that He suggested we change places,
but life has not been the same since.

When I had control
I knew the way.
It was rather boring,
but predictable...
It was the shortest distance between two points.

But when He took the lead,
He knew delightful long cuts,
up mountains,
and through rocky places
at breakneck speeds.
It was all I could do to hang on!
Even though it looked like madness,
He said, "Pedal!"

I worried and was anxious
and asked:
"Where are you taking me?"
He laughed and didn't answer,
and I started to learn to trust.

I forgot my boring life
and entered into the adventure.
And when I'd say: "I'm scared"
He'd lean back and touch my hand.

He took me to people with gifts that I needed;
gifts of healing,
acceptance
and joy.
They gave me gifts to take on my journey,
my Lord's and mine.

And we were off again.
He said: "Give the gifts away;
they're extra baggage, too much weight."
So I did
to the people we met,
and I found that in giving I received,
and still our burden was light.

I did not trust Him
at first.
in control of my life.
I thought He'd wreck it.
But he knows bike secrets;
knows how to make it bend to take sharp corners,
knows how to jump to clear high rocks,
knows how to fly to shorten scary passages.

And I am learning to shut up
and pedal
in the strangest places.
And I'm beginning to enjoy the view
and the cool breeze on my face
with my delightful constant companion,
Jesus Christ.
And when I'm sure I just can't do anymore,
He just smiles and says: ... "Pedal!"

(Author Unknown)

Paul and I retired to bed and I wrote a diary of the day's events using a special app on my phone. We gave each other a leg massage and I wondered how long we'd keep that one up. Not long, as it happened; that was the only time ever on the tour, and by 10pm we were fast asleep.

Comments / Texts

Have a great day, praying for you both, try not to fall out on the first day! Tee hee! Loads of love.

Simon

Good morning, Annie, wishing you many amazing blessings on your fantastic cycling pilgrimage. May all the saints be cycling next to you, and may your hearts be filled with joy and courage with every pedal turn.

Maz

That's a beautiful blessing and prayer, Maz, thank you! I am excited now, still can't believe we are doing this!

Annie

Golly! You must be excited, U R awake at 7am! UR never up at this time!

Maz

It's not the toothbrush that made the bolt shear off, Annie, but the 20 Dairy Milk chocolate bars we painstakingly sewed into the pannier linings so Dad wouldn't find them.
Oops, I guess he knows about them now!

Simon

Arrived safely, had cup of tea, feel human. xx

Annie (to Super 7)

Don't forget as you start your journey that we are praying for you both, also that through Christ we are forever joined in the Spirit, and therefore your joy is our joy too. Phone if you need a blessing.

Ian

Does that mean our pain is your pain too, or do we have to suffer that by ourselves?

Annie

Yes, it does, but Jude is always telling me off for being negative!

Ian

Daniel [5 years old] has just looked at the map on your flyer and said you hadn't gone very far...
says he could walk it!

Pam

O my word! I know you said Cornwall was hilly but...!
Tomorrow is twice as bad.

Annie (to Hilary)

Better pray twice as much then, hadn't I!

Hilary

Glad the first day went well – must be great cycling in the sunny Cornish weather.
Good luck on your way to Callington tomorrow – home of my secondary school and Ginsters pasties!
(Just head for the smell…)

Jason

16ᵀᴴ MAY, 2014

STAGE 2

Ponsonooth to Callington

A difficult day!

(This was not my best day on planet earth. You may want to head straight for 17th May and avoid the pain.)

The day didn't start in the best of ways when I woke early and decided to add more notes to my diary only to discover that because I hadn't pressed some silly button or other on my phone, I had lost everything I had written the night before.

Arggh! I hate technology!

Let's just all go back to pen and paper, chalk and blackboard.

I'd like to say the day improved from here but apart from a delightful breakfast with Chris and Estelle who are possibly two of the loveliest people we are ever likely to meet, it went downhill from there on in.

Or rather, uphill. *Many, many times.*

Chris asked about our route for the day and Paul took him through it. I could tell by his face that Chris thought we were mad, and when he started to talk "bus routes", I was all for asking when the next one was due. We prayed for our hosts, and they for us with our journey ahead. The way they prayed gave me an inkling that they clearly knew what we were still blissfully unaware of. Packed and ready to go, Chris suggested a different road out of Ponsonooth, as the one Paul had chosen was more of a dirt track. We really appreciated the local knowledge of all our hosts and always made use of it.

Before we left we took a photo of Chris and Estelle as we did with all our hosts. I had previously made a poster which read, "We put Paul and Annie up," on one side and, "We put up with Paul and Annie," on the other, and invited our hosts to choose. It was huge fun as the days went by and the source of much laughter and soul searching on their part as to which they should choose!

We prayed for Chris and Estelle as we climbed out of Ponsonooth and hoped we would still be as on fire for God as they were when we reached their age.

Our first unscheduled stop was in Truro. I caught a glimpse of the cathedral and insisted we stop for a photo. I had to run up a street and turn into another, and still all I got was a glimpse, but never mind. Truro seemed rather attractive and it would have been agreeable to spend the day there but the hills were calling so off we went. We rode to St Austell via Tresillian, Probus, Grampound and Hewas Water.

It would have been more straightforward to go up the A30 through Cornwall but I had heard such horrible things about it, like "squashed cyclists", that I had no intention of travelling that way. I'm nervous about any main road and so Paul's brief was to avoid them where possible, and because of that we cycled a rather tortuous route round the backroads and lanes instead.

It was all so hilly and steep that I didn't much enjoy the ride but at least the hedgerows were eye-catching; heavens above, we were going so slowly I could study them in detail and even take photos without having to dismount. I know nothing about wayside flowers but Cornwall has them in abundance; delicate pinks and all shades of blue peeping through great drifts of white, with an occasional yellow making a dramatic appearance. You don't have to know what a flower is called to appreciate its beauty, and they got me up the hills so I appreciated them all the more.

With a few miles to go before a butty stop at St Austell, our chain fell off. Depending on how the chain falls, it can be easily slipped back into place or not. When it falls between the chain wheel and frame, it makes it much harder to relocate. If it falls outwards onto the pedal, it's just a quick job to fix. (I know what I mean, even if you're confused.) Needless to say our chain fell in the difficult fashion.

By the time we got to St Austell we were both in need of food and a cuddle so we had our butties by a roundabout near a petrol station. Ian chose this moment to call,

"All you ever do is sit and have butties!"

Paul took a photo of me and posted it on the blog later that night; my sister saw it and remarked,

"She's not happy."

O, how true, and it was about to become a whole lot worse.

The journey to Liskeard was a personal nightmare, and if I wasn't enjoying it then Paul wouldn't either. We cycled for forever from St Austell through Pa, Tywardreath and Lostwithiel, where we waited at a level crossing for a train to go by. 38 carriages later we were able to carry on our journey through Fairy Cross, West Taphouse, Middle Taphouse and – yes, you guessed it – East Taphouse; on to Doublebois and then a wonderful – the *only* wonderful – run down into Liskeard where we hit 40.1mph top speed. We had to get off the bike and walk up some of the hills. There were many tears, and I honestly wondered if I would make it to the end of the day, let alone the end of the tour.

Our minister Derek – another Derek; they are like buses in my life; I don't know any for years and then two come along at once – comes from Cornwall and did warn us about the hills. I heard him but didn't hear him, if you get my drift. He did encourage me though by saying,

"Cornwall will be the worst. Don't get discouraged if you have to get off; it won't all be like that."

Anyone who's ever done LEJOG will say the same; there is something about the never-ending ups and downs of the Cornish hills that really takes it out of you. They are like dragon's teeth. And don't be fooled by the 'downs'; they last all of ten seconds after having climbed ten minutes beforehand.

I began to have a physical reaction in my stomach whenever we came to yet another hill, and felt decidedly sick. I'm sure that Cornwall is absolutely delightful – just not on a bike. It was an incredibly hot day too which didn't help matters; the best weather to cycle in is cooler temperatures but not windy; no rain, snow or traffic, and then I'm happy... ish.

Paul was finding it hard too but throughout all of this he remained upbeat and strong, mentally and physically. He had to; he had to get off and push the bike single-handedly up the hills because I couldn't even keep pace with him walking. If I could, I would choose flat roads every time on the bike. We think the same thing when we see a hill, we just use a different intonation in our heads. Paul thinks, "Oh great, a hill!" and sees it as an exciting challenge. I use the same words, but not in a happy way. I knew Paul had prepared the route for us and taken into consideration how I felt, but sometimes the only way is up, and that is how it was this day.

Instead of seeing the hills as a problem, a difficulty, I wanted to see them as an opportunity to prove how fit I had become with training over the last few months – but it was jolly hard. I kept thinking, "It's all to do with perseverance." I knew I had to flex my muscles, put them to use and work hard to get through this difficult time.

My life is often like that too; a situation arises where I can use it as an opportunity to prove God's truth in me, or sulk and whine and stamp my feet. I am learning what it is to flex my spiritual muscles, to be disciplined and put into practice what I am learning in my relationship with God, through scripture or fellowship with others. Sometimes my walk with God is mile by glorious mile, sometimes it's inch by painful inch, but I want to always move forward. That is perseverance.

Inch by inch was how it was now.

We had our second butty stop on the outskirts of Liskeard, and Derek the trucker phoned. He was very sweet and reminded me of a worship song by Matt Redman, the one about God's name being blessed on the road marked with suffering and that there is pain in the offering.

Derek and I agreed this was a great song to sing in the circumstances and we warbled together across the phone lines before we lost signal.

From Liskeard we had the long climb to Callington via Merrymeet, St Ive, Gang, Bicton Manor, and Golberdon. There were more tears, more horrible hills and a dangerous walk on the verge of the A390. One descent in Bicton was so steep we had to get off and walk that too! According to the profile of the day, the ride into Callington was going to be a bit of a pull, but thankfully it wasn't as bad as we had prepared for.

Our chain fell off again within two miles of our destination. Why do these things happen just when you really don't want them to? I phoned our host Wendy to let her know we were going to be at least another half an hour and she was very jolly indeed and said she would put the shepherd's pie in the oven when we arrived so not to worry.

Those words galvanised me into action. I love shepherd's pie.

As we cycled up the lane to their farm, we were waved down by an elderly man who wanted to talk. I really, *really* didn't, but dutifully got off the bike and had a look at his vegetable patch as instructed. In fact I ended up leaning on the wall and having quite a conversation with him.

A car drove by. It was Wendy's husband, David. He said to Paul,

"That's my dad. He has Alzheimer's."

I was so tired that I hadn't noticed.

We reached Wendy and the shepherd's pie at just gone 5pm after fifty-three miles of sheer something-never-to-be-repeated;

six hours in the saddle, plus another two for stops, tears, toilet, and butties. It had been the hardest day ever in the saddle, and we had the spectre of Dartmoor looming over us the next day.

We still managed to spend an enjoyable evening in the company of our hosts and their friend Jean, and fell into bed at around 8.30pm. Actually we fell into *beds;* we had singles for the night. We haven't slept in single beds in the same room ever and this proved to be a problem, and not the one that you might be thinking of.

Paul snores. (He says I snore as well, but I can't imagine for one minute that I do.) Usually I gently kick him or touch his tummy and he stops, but this option was not possible now so I lined up a load of missiles to throw at him during the night should he start. As it happened, we were both out like a light, and shoes, water bottles and mobile phones were still in a neat row by my bed come the morning.

Comments / Texts

Just to let you know that I feel your pain, although it has left me with a disturbing thought of you chasing Paul around a stranger's bathroom with a pot of bottom cream. Happy cycling and much blessing.

Ian

Have arrived, will blog later. Thanks for prayers.
Bin hard day. Glad to be here!

Annie (to Super 7)

I knew Dad would be in tears by day 2.
No doubt you held it together, Annie, speaking great words of encouragement from the back seat throughout the 53 miles!! Well done!!

Simon

Really glad that you are home and dry for the night.
Sweet dreams. God bless.

Shirley

Well done on a tough day – I know those roads well. Hoping and praying that tomorrow's ride into Devon goes well – beware of the hills up, down and up if you go through St Ann's Chapel and Gunnislake.

Jason

Hi Annie, I've seen you in work-out sessions, you're well up to hills… Dig out that inner ninja and keep pedalling. Sorry to hear Paul has shed tears, are you just too fit for him? Maybe sing something upbeat while you eat your butties to cheer up inner spirits.

Sally

I'm sorry you've had such a difficult day of it but thank God for the lovely people you're meeting on the way. Things will get easier (Derek did warn you about the start) and I'm sure you'll be able to look back on your first days with a smile once you get further north. Take care and remember all those people who are praying for you and willing you on.

Geoff and Claire

17TH MAY, 2014

STAGE 3

Callington to Exeter

Out on the wild and windy moor...

Considering we felt we had the climb of our lives ahead of us, we both woke in an exceptionally good mood, though I still doused myself in Forever to mark the enormity of what lay before us.

All our hosts wanted to cook us huge breakfasts. I can understand why they did, but I can't face cooked food at the beginning of the day and Paul isn't a big eater either, so every day on the tour we had to let our hosts down gently and just have cereal.

We left Wendy and David at around 9am and only got to the top of the lane before we went through the other daily conversation:

"Did you remember to pack the bottom cream?"

"Yes, what about my glasses?"

"Yes, what about mine?"

"Maybe we should just stop and check…"

Derek rang early that day to make sure I was in a better mood, and that we were continuing on course and had not thrown in the towel.

I was.

We hadn't.

All was good in our world, though to be fair we'd only been cycling for about half an hour at this point.

Our first main climb, which we mostly scaled on hands and knees, was through Gunnislake. It lies in a dip between two steep hills; think of a shark's tooth and you have the profile of Gunnislake. From there we journeyed to Tavistock and stopped to rest for food and drink. We were learning that little and often was the best way; for our bottoms if nothing else. Heading in to Tavistock we passed a huge church tower that dwarfed the houses next to it and did a pretty good fancy dress as a Cape Canaveral rocket.

In buoyant mood I strode into a local shop to buy bananas and in conversation with the assistant told her our plans. The whole shop came alive with everyone wishing us well and saying they were glad it was us and not them.

Mmm… I wasn't sure what to make of that.

We knew the climb ahead would be hard so we had our first energy drink to fortify us and I decided that whenever the going was really tough or we had to walk, I would do something positive and pray for people.

I prayed a lot that day.

We climbed from three hundred feet in Tavistock to the top of Dartmoor at over fifteen hundred. As we walked up a particularly steep bit, two riders went by on single bikes carrying no luggage. (I refer to cyclists like this as "day trippers".)

I applauded as they passed us by on their way up and Paul called out to them,

"Well done! I would join you if I wasn't carrying all this weight," pointing in my general direction. He will forever claim that he meant the panniers.

Eventually we too summited, just as a driver went by on the other side of the road. He hooted and did a thumbs up and at that moment it was the best feeling ever. I felt we had climbed Everest together. We were so pleased and kept congratulating each other and even though we'd had to get off a few times, we were exhilarated. I couldn't imagine being there with anyone else but Paul. We had achieved so much together on this journey and it seemed a reflection of our marriage too. As we stood side by side it was as moving as standing before the minister twenty years previously, but now we had all those years of memories gluing us together; a shared history, children and grandchildren. I got a bit soppy then.

You may be doing the maths and thinking, "How come they have two married sons and grandchildren after just twenty years? That's good going in anyone's book."

Let me explain. Jamie and Simon are Paul's boys from his first marriage. I took them on when they were young teenagers. I love them as my own, and their growing families.

It's an attitude of heart, not biology.

We heard what I thought was a cuckoo so I named a nearby outcrop Cuckoo Rock (and took yet another photo). We had imagined the top of Dartmoor to be flat but in reality it was full of all the ups and downs we had come to know and... well... *know*. It was like cycling across the top of the world and as we rode along chatting away and enjoying the barren beauty and the cooler weather, the chain came off.

Aarrgghh!

Fortunately we were close to a lay-by so we ducked in, and while Paul got his hands dirty, I phoned Ian and Jude to tell them of our triumph. Jude is one of my closest friends and I wanted to share the moment with her, but she was shopping in Manchester so I only had Ian to talk to. He was nonetheless duly impressed and at least I wasn't eating at the time.

A car pulled in and when we spoke to the people about our tour they gave us money for the charities. Can you believe it? On the top of Dartmoor and we were receiving donations!

Our Dartmoor excursion took us through Merrivale, Princetown, Two Bridges and Postbridge. Descending into Moreton-hampstead, we stopped for a coffee and sat on a public bench in the middle of the town with five lads sitting opposite. It turned out they were doing their bronze Duke of Edinburgh award which, they told us, was "hard graft". When we told them we were doing Land's End to John O' Groats, we were given "serious respect, man".

I wanted to rush over and high-five each one of them but thought it might scare them, and restrained myself from any show of spontaneity that could be misinterpreted as madness.

It happens to me. A lot.

I hadn't studied the profile of the day's route properly that morning at breakfast and thought there was no more climbing after Dartmoor so went into serious shock with a jolly steep climb out of Moretonhampstead. From there we made our way to Exeter.

I had previously decided that every time we entered a new county I would get off the bike and take a photo of the signboard, but it's such a lot of hassle stopping, then both of us having to unclip our shoes from the pedals, getting off the tandem, finding my phone, taking a photo and then doing the whole thing again in reverse, that I gave up that idea before we ever passed from the first to the second. It happened somewhere before Moretonhampstead, I think.

On the outskirts of Exeter our chain came off again.

Paul fixed it.

We cycled twenty yards or so farther and the blessed thing came off again.

Something was definitely wrong and Paul knew he would have to examine it closely when we stopped for the day. I took the opportunity to have a toilet stop and ducked behind a bush near a builder's site for a quick wee only to look up and see a CCTV camera trained directly on me.

O the shame.

We gingerly continued our journey praying that the chain would hold. Even if it did, Mr White-van-man wanted to play his part in making our journey as precarious as possible by pulling out right in front of us and nearly forcing us off the road.

Bless.

Once in Exeter we went along the embankment by the river Ex. I wasn't at all convinced cyclists were allowed to do this.

"Malcolm says we can," said Paul like a petulant five-year-old.

Oh well, if Malcolm says… Would that hold up with the local police, I wondered?

Shirley was genuinely surprised when we knocked on the door.

"You are expecting us, aren't you?" – a little worried she had entirely forgotten.

She was, but not for another two hours.

That made my day.

We have visited Exeter several times since half the family moved there and know the locality, which served Paul well now as he knew there was a bike shop to hand.

"Our chain is kinky; we need a new one," he said.

There was an awful lot I could have said in response to that but let it pass.

We had cycled forty-seven miles that day and every inch was printed on our ever increasingly sensitive behinds. My hands were suffering too even though I wore cycling gloves, and I had the beginnings of blisters appearing at the base of the 'v' between thumb and forefinger.

(I know you're looking, aren't you?)

Shirley and Malcolm had invited their eldest son Matt and his wife Anna to share the evening meal. They were the young couple who had done LEJOG last summer and had inspired us to do the same. For this fact alone, I wasn't sure whether to kick them or hug them.

I plumped for a hug.

It was so good to exchange stories with them and we all discussed in detail the highs and the lows over one or three bottles of jolly good wine. It was reassuring to know that they understood when we said "Gunnislake" with a wry grin, or "St Austell to Liskeard" with a twitch in one eye. They are LEJOG veterans and knew where we had come from.

And where we were going.

Paul had to drag me to bed that night. I was enjoying myself far too much with the family, the stories, the laughter, the wine…

Comments / Texts

Praying for you even on a Saturday!

Ian

Arrived safe, great day on Dartmoor, loads better than yesterday. Thanx for prayers and encouragement!

Annie (to Super 7)

Another night, another guest bed…

Annie (to Charlotte)

We are following your route on the map and praying for you every day – delighted that today was better for you. As to the chain problem – you are in good company with our Methodist forefathers. Charles Wesley wrote in verse four of 'And Can It Be',
"My chains fell off, my heart was free,
I rose, went forth, and followed Thee."
Geoff Phillips calls this hymn "the biker's song".
Seriously, take care of each other on this great adventure (we are sure you will).
Take care and God bless!

John and Margaret

Re: the blog photo. How comes dad looks more tired than you, Annie? Just proves your fitness far exceeds his! Well done on today's achievement.

Simon

The scenery looks breathtaking, you both must feel a great sense of achievement making all the peddling worthwhile.

Margaret

Have been singing 'One More Pedal' for you, praying and thinking of you both so much. Looking forward to seeing you tonight in Exeter. Bless you both.

Mum

Good to see that fuller than full smile back again from you, Annie, and so impressed that it was highs all the way today (apart from the shark's tooth!) Enjoy being with your family tonight, both of you, and we will be praying with you all the 50 or so miles tomorrow! God bless, love to all in Exeter and good night. xxxx

Jude

18TH MAY, 2014

STAGE 4

Exeter to Pawlett

Like a walk in the park.

Inspired by our last three days of climbing...

Paul decided to wear his Tour de France 'King of the mountains' cycling shirt; it's white with big red dots all over it and I told him he looked like Pudsey Bear on a training exercise.

Inspired by our last three days of climbing...

I was thanking God that today was a relatively flat stage. I knew it was going to be desperately hard to leave my family in Exeter and dragged my feet for as long as possible but had to face the inevitable and get on the bike again.

Ouch! Everything hurt.

We both liberally assaulted our behinds with cream. (By the end of the tour we were putting it on morning, noon and night, we were that saddle sore.) Malcolm decided my hands were in need of some protection too and taped them up with some incredibly sticky stuff but it did the trick; nothing was going to rub and make my blisters worse. I did vaguely wonder how I was going to get the tape off at the end of the day without ripping my hands to shreds but decided that was tonight's problem and I had a shed-load of others to face before then; about fifty miles of them.

Before we left, Malcolm smothered me in sun cream too. (I think I was his little project; he was definitely proud of his little sister-in-law and I loved the care he showed.) We prayed together as a family and then departed. Malcolm joined us for a mile or so on his own bike and was appalled to see Paul go straight through some red lights. Believe me, so was I. Paul's way of explanation was that it was early and there was no traffic coming in the other direction and...

"It's such a faff to unclip, re-balance, set off and clip back in again that I thought it would be OK."

I made it clear that in future it would not be OK.

OK?

Paul had put a new chain on the bike the night before and had given it a once over adjusting the cables etc. with Malcolm helping. Paul is a bit of a control freak when it comes to his bikes. He has three bikes but only one bottom – go figure! – and likes to do it all himself. If Malcolm was even allowed to touch the wheel or hold a spanner, he should consider himself blessed. Anyway, everything today was working well and all seemed tickety-boo!

We rode through Broadclyst and Mutterton to our first butty stop at Culmstock which was really very pleasant indeed. We had ordered jam butties for Paul; ham, lettuce and cucumber for me; and Shirley had provided. Each day our hosts sent us off with a packed lunch and we never had two days the same. I have a friend Geoff who has the same sandwiches, Primula cheese spread, every day at work, five days a week, every week of the year excluding holidays.

Lord, save me!

We found a bench for my whole body to lie down on, which was bliss in comparison to one very achy part of me in the saddle. I made the most of it and took my gloves, helmet and shoes off and lay there wishing I could teleport to John O' Groats to cheer Paul in when he arrived.

Derek phoned, which was nice because it was a Sunday and I didn't expect him to. Both Paul and I were in a good mood but the last three days had quite taken it out of us and we were tired. We had a few hills today but in comparison to Cornwall it was a breeze.

Our second stop was at the Monkton Arms near Taunton for a latte and more butties. It was another super-hot day so it was a joy to find shade under a wooden pagoda type thing. Paul is not a cat lover but they seem to love him and a beautiful black one plonked itself on the seat right next to him for the duration. I am assuming it was Paul it was keen on, but it might have had a secret love for strawberry jam, I'll never know. It didn't get any, I do know that much. Paul was sharing his sandwiches with nobody. Never.

From there we cycled to our hosts at Pawlett, just south of Bristol. We had a hairy moment cycling through Bridgewater involving a car. The problem of being on a bike in traffic, and a long bike at that (the tandem is about 8ft) is that some car drivers are impatient and try to beat us to the lights, round corners or, in this case, to the island in the road and beyond.

The driver realized he wouldn't make it without hitting us and slammed on his brakes. Sitting on the back of the bike I saw all this happen in vivid technicolour as he and I eyeballed each other, and I felt deeply compelled to point out the error of his ways to him in no uncertain terms; and on a Sunday too.

Bridgewater boasts a canal and as narrow boating is another love Paul and I share, I insisted once again in getting off the bike to take a photo; it looked so idyllic.

When we cycle, Paul has low handlebars and with his head down he just concentrates on the road ahead; no bad thing. I, on the other hand, sit straight in the saddle and spend the time enjoying the scenery. I've been known to eat chocolate or text a friend without Paul being any the wiser.

I just have to sit on the back and pedal.

But I do pedal.

Today was the first day on the tour we heard the words we have so often heard in the past:

"She's not pedalling at the back!"

It's quite comical because everyone who says this either thinks this is a completely original thought to them, or that it's a little 'in joke' that they're sharing with us.

Ha ha.

Most of the time I take it good-naturedly, however, just to put the record straight: (!)

The front and back pedals are joined by a single chain, so I have to pedal at the same rate as Paul. I can do no other, unless I unclip of course and let my legs hang loose, but that would really knock us off balance, and on a tandem balance is vital. Years ago there was a P. G. Tips advert with two chimps on a bike and one says to the other,

"Can yer ride tandem?"

Believe me, there is an art to it; you have to work together or it just won't work at all.

When we borrowed our first ever tandem from friends, we had to pick it up from Bollington, about five miles from where we lived; so we took our son Simon with us, and he and Paul rode the tandem home whilst I followed behind in the car. Watching them fall off for the third time, I thought, "If Paul thinks I'm getting on that, he's got another think coming."

The problem arose because they were each strong cyclists doing their own thing and on a tandem both parties have to work in unison, not separately. On our bike I have no brake, no gears, no control of steering; I just have to sit there and do what Paul says. "Pedal." "Stop." Paul says it's the only time in our marriage I do what I'm told so he likes to make the most of it.

If you are a man and want to be the head of the house, take your wife out on a tandem. Borrow ours if you'd like.

I've thought a great deal about this idea of balance as I've sat on the back of the bike and related it to my life as a Christian.

There's a verse in the Bible that pretty much says the same thing:

"Since you live by the Spirit, keep in step with the Spirit." (Galatians 5:25)

I've come to realize as a Christian that I need to work with God; not fight him, try to run ahead of him, or do my own thing. When I keep in step with him, I stay spiritually balanced; when I try my own methods – go my own way, push too hard or conversely don't bother – I become unbalanced in my spiritual thinking and that has a negative knock-on effect in my daily life.

Speaking of balance, I have an ornament on our mantelpiece: a duck holding two cakes and with a sign round its neck saying, "A balanced life is a cake in each hand."

That works well for me too.

We arrived hot and happy but exhausted, just after 3pm, to a cheery welcome from Muriel and Mike.

Before we started the tour we sent letters to each of our hosts outlining our goals and our daily requirements. Part of it read:

"Annie eats anything except Brussels sprouts and Paul is allergic to cheese."

So when Mike announced shortly after our arrival, "Are the Brussels in the fridge dear? I've still got to top them with melted cheddar," and winked at me, I knew we were home.

Mike turned out to be quite a card. When I still hadn't materialized dressed and fresh after nearly an hour upstairs, he remarked to Paul,

"It's awfully quiet up there. I hope Annie hasn't cycled all this way just to drown in the bath."

I was fast asleep on the bed.

While Muriel cooked us a great roast dinner with all the trimmings (which was an exceptionally good thing as we were ravenous), we took a walk round their delightful garden. It was so pleasant to have the time and space to relax and do something that I enjoy so much.

Unfortunately, we didn't have the energy to stay up beyond half past eight, and bade them goodnight.

We had ridden fifty miles and spent only four and a half hours in the saddle, *and* we didn't get off to walk up a hill once – a first for us.

Comments / Texts

We've just sung, "...my chains fell off..." at church.
Hope yours hasn't!

Hilary

Arrived safe, will blog later,
tired in this heat but happy.

Annie (to Super 7)

Loving the blog, the photos, and especially Paul's 'King
of the mountains' spotty shirt. Go, Annie, on the re-
educating car drivers front! Keep hydrated in this
sizzling weather and take care through Bristol, my
home town. God bless.

Bev and Andy

You are H-A-P-P-Y,
you are H-A-P-P-Y.
You know you are,
you're sure you are,
you are H-A-P-P-Y.
I was thinking Paul has a look of Pudsey Bear
about him with all those spots.
His smile, however, could knock spots off Pudsey!

Jude

Great to hear things are tickety-boo now.
Hope you're not overheating in lovely weather!

Geoff and Claire

Pippa & Jack[2] have just looked at their world map and stated: "Granny and Grandad haven't got far to go, why won't we see them for another 2 weeks?"
Oh to think like a child!
They send you lots of kisses and cuddles!

Simon

Glad you're progressing & that today's been a breeze compared to Cornwall! We did warn you!!! Keep those legs going up & down so the wheels go round & round – every pedal push means one less to go! Sending love.

Hilary

---

[2] Pippa and Jack are seven and five respectively

19ᵀᴴ MAY, 2014

STAGE 5
Pawlett to Thornbury

"What are you whinging about, woman?"

These words were not uttered by Paul, who knows better than to stick his head in the lion's mouth and say, "Chew."

These words were spoken by Ian on the phone at a very safe distance.

At the time we were sitting by the roadside in Clevedon by yet another petrol station drinking a Costa Coffee, and I was not a happy bunny. I wanted sympathy; what I got was the above. But it made me laugh.

Eventually.

The day had started so well with breakfast at Mike and Muriel's. They are a lovely couple in their eighties, and I wanted to adopt them on the spot. Over tea and toast Mike re-lived his days of cycling as a young man on the continent following the 'Tour de France' route. I looked over at Paul and saw a gleam in his eye that sent shivers up my spine.

"Forget it, it's not happening," I warned him, breadknife in hand.

I would have been happy to stay all day with M and M, pottering about the garden, but Paul said, "On yer bike," and that was that.

We had a false start and nearly fell off, which is always embarrassing with people watching, and then headed straight into a headwind for the first hour or so.

One of the first villages we passed through that morning was Mark. The signpost was so huge and unavoidable that I decided that maybe God was nudging me to pray for a friend of mine with the same name. After the tour I told my friend Mark about the incident. He told me that Monday was the day that he and his wife had gone through a very traumatic experience and he was comforted with the thought that God had impressed on others the need to pray.

God, you are incredible! You organise the troops and get us praying for each other even when it's not our business to know the reasons why.

It's a part of true fellowship that can never be counterfeited.

Paul had discovered the most attractive cycle route called 'The Strawberry Line' which led us round the outskirts of Cheddar Gorge and Axbridge. It was an ideal place to sit and have our first butty stop. Our bodies were going through the pain barrier today and everything hurt. I had managed to soak off the sticky strips on my hands the night before and hadn't needed to reapply them in the morning. If only they made something like that for backsides; painful to remove, I shouldn't wonder, but I live in hope of one day sitting on a saddle and enjoying a pain-free existence.

I have got through six saddles so far in my quest to find the perfect fit. I've often said to Paul that something akin to an armchair would be ideal and, to be fair, my current saddle is probably the closest I can get without Paul becoming suspicious. He sits on a saddle that is the stuff of nightmares; long, hard and narrow. Paul's saddle is five inches wide whereas mine is nine inches wide and deeply padded; it needs to be, it has a large derrière to accommodate. The seat-post on the back of a tandem has suspension built into it which is supposed to help – and probably does, except on the front of a tandem you don't bounce about but on the back it's like a bucking bronco.

The cushioning effect of the saddle and the suspension help.

Slightly.

For a supposedly flat day it was proving very hilly so by the time we hit Clevedon life was bleak. I cracked and asked Paul for chocolate to help the coffee go down and he must have realized I was in a bad way because he returned with a family size bag of Minstrels.

We hadn't heard from Ian that day so I sent a sad little text:

"Am sat by roadside at petrol station in Clevedon having a coffee and a bit of a downer. Please pray, it's 56 miles today and everything hurts."

Any decent human being would respond with encouraging words, sympathy, and an up-lifting message.

Ian phoned straightaway and his opening line was,

"What are you whinging about, woman?"

Even Paul took a deep breath and stepped away from me.

Re-invigorated by coffee, chocolate and those moving words from my now ex-friend, we set off again, and Derek phoned shortly after. He came supplied with a whole dictionary of encouraging words and helpfully explained that our bodies were going through a "What the heck are you playing at?" rebellious phase, and would acclimatize soon when they realized this was how life was going to be for the foreseeable future. He and I agreed that the worst was over – sorry, Cornwall! – and the midlands would give Paul and me time to recuperate before we hit the next big climbs in Cumbria. We also agreed that Ian didn't have a sympathetic bone in his body, but someone had to be his friend and the lot fell on us.

Even though Paul was following his GPS route, we got lost in Pill. Technology led us through a housing estate and would have taken us through someone's front room had we stuck to it. We were tired, we were aching, and were getting a tinsy-winsy bit lost and a tinsy-winsy bit fretful. Just as we were getting a tinsy-winsy bit murderous with each other, God sent a guide-ian angel along in the form of a fellow cyclist, Norman, who met us on the cycle track next to the M5 and led us safely across the bridge and heading in the right direction for Thornbury. This gave us both time to calm down, and shortly after we had our second butty stop and used it as another opportunity to water this green and pleasant land. (By the time we got to John O' Groats we were experts at pulling down our lycra in the most unlikely of places. Shirley and Malcolm did suggest I call this book "Wild Weeing" in recognition of all the hills, valleys, tunnels, roadsides and farmers' fields that we used as toilets au naturelle.)

Whilst writing this book I obviously read it out to Paul for any comments he may have. His comment just now was,

"It was great, wasn't it? Doesn't it just make you want to do it all again?"

And I thought he understood me...

We had cycled forty-six miles that day and still had another twelve to go to reach our destination; they went by laboriously and achingly slow. A friend had commented to me weeks before just how hard it would be at the end of each day; we would have to make conversation with our new hosts and be terribly polite even if we weren't feeling like it, when all we would want to do would be to shower, eat and sleep. I did wonder how I would cope on our arrival this night. Previously, adrenaline had always kicked in, and whenever we had arrived at our hosts I was just so thankful for their hospitality that I wanted to bless them as much as they had already blessed us. But five days under our belt and I was tired and in pain, and just wanted *my* bed and *my* pillow.

We arrived at Pete and Debs around 4.30pm. As we rode exhausted and relieved into their driveway, I saw Debs leap up from her chair to answer the door. She was so sweet and, in a way, *excited* to see us that once again we felt enveloped by good people whom we knew would care for us that night. It's incredibly humbling to receive so much from people without being able to give anything in return; and they gave freely and easily. Debs in particular had been following our progression on the blog so had a good idea of our journey and our characters.

Paul's bout with flu had left him with an infection in his left ear due to a build-up of gunk and stuff (you don't want to know) and he couldn't hear properly. After securing the bike in the garage he walked into the house and literally started shouting at Pete, who must have thought, "Who is this deranged lunatic yelling at me?" but instead he just smiled and nodded in all the right places. Paul was explaining something or other about the day and it is the only time in my life when I have had to ask him to lower his voice. There is only room for one fog-horn in this family, Paul, and it isn't you.

It is amazing how quickly we can recover once we have had a bath and freshened up; new clothes, brushed teeth, slippers, a cup of tea and a good meal. Tonight was no exception and we had a thoroughly enjoyable evening discussing the light-hearted things of life as well as serious theology. I think it was something to do with Pete's Ph.D. on fractals and the new expression of church.

Or maybe it was the church expressing new facts about fractals.

I can't remember.

I had had wine.

I did remember that Pete was a Methodist minister though so I tried really hard to behave.

Once again Paul had to drag me to bed. In another life that could have been a whole heap of fun; as it was, we were asleep as soon as our heads hit the pillow.

Comments / Texts

Hi Paul and Annie,
It's good that you are on the flat now and today should be better going. But thinking on the positive side, Annie, you should have built up your leg muscles like a top athlete. In fact by now you should be able to crack nuts with your thighs. Well at least Jude and I will know where to come at Christmas. Happy cycling!

Ian

Arrived shattered, will blog later.

Annie (to Super 7)

Keep going, you're doing fantastically well. I'm sure you're right; God really did send His guardian angel to guide you, and He'll lift you up when the going gets tough. "Underneath are the everlasting arms." Always in our prayers.

Jim

Quarter of the way (in days... not looked at miles)... Woohoo! Well done u. The uphill struggles make the downhills a greater blessing! See u in 2 sleeps... Brussels sprouts with cheese sauce awaits you!

Pam

Annie – we heard a rumour that Astbury Garden Centre (your second home) were thinking of laying off some staff until you returned as the number of regular customers was much reduced at present!

John and Margaret

I am so pleased you have arrived as Ian had told me you were in real pain with blisters etc.
We are up at Wellspring tonight so I will encourage all to send up arrow prayers through the days and nights until you have made it to the top!
What a great God – how many angels has He sent dressed in luminous green geotex and riding a bike? One day you will be able to ask Him!
Ian is sitting next to me (who appears to be rather familiar with those encouraging words on your blog header!) and is much amused – but much pleased that you are feeling positive for Day 6. You now have a blog link, courtesy of Jason, from the church home page slide show – it is very impressive! Blessing to you both and to your lovely hosts.

Jude (and Ian)

That's not the first time you've got lost whilst using a GPS is it, Dad? I dread to think where you'd be if you were relying on map and compass like the time you got us lost in the hills of Yorkshire !

Simon

Lost! Just take the motorway!
Seriously, though, so you are both doing fantastically,
especially in this heat!
God love and guide you.

Helen

20TH MAY, 2014

STAGE 6

Thornbury to Evesham

The friendly hills of the shires.

We were up 'n out 'n at 'em before 9am, only to discover that the hills of Gloucestershire and Worcestershire do not need full frontal attacks; they are pleasant and graceful and rolling and green. This doesn't mean that I had grown to like them or that everything went to plan however.

After cycling up one hill Paul said, "Oh, sorry, we shouldn't have done that," and we had to turn round and head back down again.

D'oh!

I had spoken at Bosley Methodist church several months previously and may have mentioned our planned tandem ride once or twice. After the service a lovely lady, Ruth, had approached me with the brilliant suggestion that when on the tour we came to our home in Bosley for the night, she and the ladies of the church would love to cook a meal for us and a few friends. I heard the word 'food' and that was all that was needed to persuade me. I think she mentioned it being a time of encouragement to us halfway through the tour, that we could invite our friends, that it would be lovely to see us, I'm not sure; I was still concentrating on the 'f' word.

Since that conversation, the number of friends hoping to join us was growing so I thought I ought to contact her and her husband Alec just to check that feeding the five thousand was what they had intended. We had cycled about seventeen miles and were heading along the A38 towards Gloucester when the weather turned, and whilst we stopped to put on our brand new rain-proof jackets, I took the opportunity to phone Ruth.

Alec answered the call and was delighted to hear to from me, and that in itself put a smile on my face and a giggle in my heart. Even before the tour had officially started our friends and family were behind us; rooting for us and encouraging us. Every day the blogs and texts we received confirmed what we suspected all along; we were blessed with wonderful friends who truly did love us and were willing us up the country.

As the tour progressed we became more and more aware that we were supported in a bubble of prayer. We were held in people's heads and hearts. The tour had started out as a challenge for the two of us but had grown and taken a different shape entirely as more and more people got on board and shared our days; our high and our low points. We may have been the only two on the tandem but there were many more people making the journey with us.

Alec said there was room for about thirty for the meal; I knew a lot of our friends would be attending the 'Street Pastors' launch in Congleton on that night instead so thirty seemed a reasonable number. He also asked if we could stop off at the primary school in Bosley when we passed through just so the children could see the tandem. Sounded good to us, so we said yes and would work out details nearer the time. That was for Friday, today was Tuesday.

It was good going through the morning; the wind was behind us and there were no problems. Our route had taken us through farmland, with all its associated cun'ree smells, to Berkeley, and on to Slimbridge missing the beer festival by one month and Chris Packam and Springwatch by one year, but we enjoyed the memories nonetheless – of Springwatch, not the beer festival! – then up the A38 to Hardwicke and beyond.

And then we hit Gloucester.

I do not like cycling through towns, cities even less. To date Gloucester is the worst town I have had the pleasure of cycling through. I'm sure the people are lovely but *by gum!* The road system was a nightmare, to me at any rate.

Paul had to suffer me saying, "I don't like this. Which lane, which lane? What are we supposed to be doing? I still don't like this," for the duration so he probably didn't enjoy it much either.

Even so, I saw the cathedral somewhere on the left and insisted on taking a photo, which meant the usual palaver of unclipping our shoes from the pedals, getting off, running along a back-street and trying to get a half decent shot. I got a shot but it wasn't half decent; there was a dilapidated building in the foreground with a little bit of the cathedral behind. So much for my photo album.

Sigh.

We had cycled for nearly thirty miles by now, and were in that tetchy stage with each other that can only be bridged by an offering of food, so we stopped near Twigworth at a local pub for a very acceptable latte and had our first butties. Of all the moments in the universe, this was the one when Ian decided to phone. How does he do it? How does he know? Does he have a built in butty-stop radar? These are the questions that kept me awake at night. He suggested that we rename the adventure, The Great Big Tandem Teashop Tour.

From there we skirted round Cheltenham where we cycled past an Evans Cycles Superstore. No, it means nothing to me either, but Paul was in seventh heaven; he buys a lot of stuff from them apparently. I've often caught him late at night on the computer looking furtively at pictures of you-know-what.

Bikes.

Evans are responsible.

We are both insured with CTC (Cyclists Touring Club) and they send a monthly magazine about bikes to feed his vice. I think this is Paul's version of a 'lads' mag'.

On through Bishop's Cleeve, Gotherington, and Gretton, where we had our second butty stop, and on to Sedgeberrow. Paul's left hip was hurting quite badly so I placed my hand on his left bum cheek and prayed loudly so he could hear.

"Lord, take this pain away."

Not sure what the pedestrian we passed made of that.

At every traffic light, end of road, photo call, scheduled or unscheduled stop, Paul had to unclip his left shoe from the pedal and put his foot to the ground. I would counteract the imbalance by leaning slightly to the right. On his left hip he was therefore carrying his own weight, the bike, the panniers and me; it's a lot to ask of any hip.

Somewhere on this day's journey I remember we passed what looked like a Tudor style house standing about two feet off the ground, supported underneath on stone mushroom-shaped plinths. I have Googled this endlessly since but to no avail. I could have imagined the whole thing but I think not.

Answers on a postcard please.

As we rode along Paul said to me,

"I've asked Simon to get two new tyres for when we get to Bosley, so we can change them halfway up the country, just for good measure."

"Did you ask for the right size?" I replied in all seriousness – like Paul would ask for tractor tyres, honestly!

Sometimes I just can't help myself.

Coming into Evesham on the A418 was a bit hairy too. A white van driver – it had to be, didn't it? – clearly thought we would take forever to reach him and so pulled out in front of us from a side road, causing us to break sharply.

Lord, bless that driver with a little more wisdom! You know who they are.

Derek the trucker phoned briefly and we had the conversation that all road users have at some point about cars and bikes, and who is the nuisance of the two.

He had a point.

I had a point.

They were different points.

We arrived in Hartington, just outside Evesham and the home of my Aunt Sheila and Uncle Dennis, having notched up another fifty-eight miles in the saddle. Dennis took one look at us and suggested we catch the bus the next day.

I should have had a much longer soak in the bath but I could hear hoots of laughter coming from the dining room and didn't want to miss out; Sheila and Dennis are naturally funny people and together they are a winning team. I love them dearly and it was a real joy to spend time with them.

Sheila did us proud with a chicken casserole, followed by strawberries and cream *and* chocolate brownies, happily helped down by a good bottle of white.

I love that woman.

Despite the free entertainment, exhaustion kicked in and once again after fulfilling our blog and diary duties we were fast asleep by 9pm.

Comments / Texts

Thinkin of u on stage 6. Hope u don't get too wet in the rain we've been havin. Keep on goin' – we believe in u!

Jamie

Arrived about an hour ago!
Safe and happy to be here! Am in bath relaxing.
Paul showered and drinking coffee, all very civilised!

Annie (to super 7)

Love from Mums n Tots. We sang "wheels on the bus, and pedals on the tandem, bell on the tandem, Paul and Annie on the tandem" today!
God bless u all day long! xx

Joan

Hello, gorgeous girlie, and her dashing sidekick!
I have just read your blog and it's FAB, wow, it sounds an amazing ride! Well done so far TEAM ROEBUCK!!
Sending you both gallons of love and hi energy chocolaty kisses!! Wish I was perched on the handlebars with sumthing 2 record your conversations during those uphill moments!!
Love you lots xoxoxoxoxo

Maz

It's another day and another 50 miles but what a joy to be doing this in the Lord Jesus Christ, please be assured he is with you every turn of the pedal, which makes me wonder... Do you actually stop pedalling in your sleep, Annie, or do you wake up when you hear Paul hit the floor? He'll be black and blue I'll bet. Anyway there'll be no tears today as it's sprouts for tea. They could work in your favour if only Annie has them. You could get her, Paul, to stand up on the pedals then light the blue touch paper and you'll fly! Praise the Lord and praise to you two.

Ian

!!**+!?**!!#+*?!

Annie

No, I don't know how to spell f**t either. Haha!

Ian

Re: the blog photo, I am sure you look much slimmer, Annie? It's all the help you are giving Paul.

Rhona

2 tractor tyres waiting for you at Stoneyfold. That is what you asked for, wasn't it?

Simon

Hi there. We all had a look at your blog in the classroom yesterday. Jack was visibly proud of you both and answered lots of questions from the children. Keep up the good work.

Grandson Jack's infant school teacher

Hello Mrs Cole, hello Jack's class, hello Jack!
Lovely to hear from you, and know that you have been following our blog! We are really enjoying cycling up the country (but our bottoms are a bit sore from sitting on the saddle so long!)
Do you think we are too old to do this?! You are never too old to take on an adventure!
Today we are going to Rugby to stay with Jack's cousins Daniel and Joseph.
Have a super half term, all of you. Enjoy riding your bikes in the park or round the garden. Remember to always wear a helmet and watch out carefully for danger, to avoid it! Stay safe!
Lots of love, Jack's Granny and Grandad xxx

Annie (written the following day)

You are both inspirational... Well done on doing so well, I think all the preparation is paying off.
Will continue to watch your progress and pray for lots of flat roads with no cars

Julia

Congratulations on day 6, do you get a Sabbath rest tomorrow? Excellent to have added a few more counties to your collection, presumably Herefordshire and Worcestershire today.
You seem to be getting quicker!

Malcolm

21ST MAY, 2014

STAGE 7

Evesham to Rugby

Part timers r us!

We had a great night's sleep in the guest bedroom, surrounded by Sheila's art and craft stuff. I was tempted to go on a 'reccy' but tiredness held me down with invisible chains and I couldn't leave the bed.

We woke to celebrate Sheila's birthday. We arranged for flowers to be delivered later in the day. Then after an enjoyable breakfast – the food and the company – we made our corned beef and delicious chutney sandwiches and set off just after 9am. This was only after the obligatory photo call with Dennis poised ready to mount the saddle and pedal off into the morning sun bolstered up with every drug possible to keep his arthritis, bad knees, blood pressure, whatever at bay.

"Eat your heart out, Lance Armstrong," I thought. "Dennis is on a legal high."

We made really good time cycling twenty-five miles in the first hour and a half. Believe me, with all that we were carrying, that was really good time! At one point we hit over 40mph going downhill; it felt so fast I thought we were in danger of getting to the bottom of the hill and up the other side before the bike did, the momentum was that strong.

We headed towards Rugby and our grandchildren in fine spirit; the weather was beautiful and the ride itself was bliss (almost).

We travelled along the Fosse Way, which is a bit up and downy like Cornwall, but not as drastic.

The Fosse Way has existed since Roman times and links Exeter to Lincoln in a fairly straight road. We stopped for our inevitable butty stop near Moreton Paddox and I waxed lyrical at how thrilling it was to be travelling along this ancient highway, imagining all the other people throughout the ages who had made the same journey.

Years ago when I was at Cliff College and on a church mission to Cornwall – I liked it back then – I stayed in a four hundred year old farmhouse in St Germaine. To open the kitchen door you had to put your finger through a hole and lift the wooden peg up on the other side. The door was original to the house, and every time I put my finger through the hole I thought of all the other fingers throughout its existence doing the same. I love that sense of living history. I find it quite dynamic.

The texts and blogs we received during the tour kept our spirits high and today was no exception. Our niece Natalie wrote that she was enjoying our blog so much that when we got to John O' Groats, could we please turn round and cycle back down the country.

My initial thought remains unprintable.

I wrote in the blog later that night, "...Let's just think about this for a minute... No!"

The English do not mince their words; if a road is called Windmill Hill Lane, you can count on three things: it's a *lane* up a *hill* with a *windmill* on it. So when we ventured up Windmill Hill Lane near Chesterton we thought we knew it all. What we didn't count on was the spectacular view it offered us. We rode up it to be rewarded with a beautiful scene of a windmill – no surprise there – in a field of bright yellow rapeseed. The fencing and trees along the edge served to add more colour and contrast to the scene. The powder blue sky held pretty puffy clouds and the wind was warm on our faces. We dismounted and breathed it all in, only speaking occasionally in happy companionship; it was one of those special moments in the tour. (That said, I've just read this back to Paul and although he remembers the moment, it isn't in his top ten. So much for sharing the experience then!)

Now in Warwickshire and ticking off the counties as we went, we were in Shakespeare country and, as Ian pointed out to me, one of his greatest works was written here: "Alas poor Warwick, I knew him well."

I know, its rough.

After 49 miles, less than four hours in the saddle and several butty stops, we arrived in Clifton-Upon-Dunsmore, just outside Rugby, at 2pm, in time to shower and change and pick our grandson Daniel up from school.

It was our best time to date; maybe I was developing cycling legs after all, or maybe it was just because it was a flat day.

Whatever, I was glad to be there and enjoying the tour enormously now. A friend has told me that cycling in the Loire valley in France is pretty – and pretty flat too. I may put it on my bucket list, and cross off the Himalayas on Paul's.

We took a barging holiday once from Rose Narrow Boats in Clifton-Upon-Dunsmore and enjoyed a brilliant week navigating the Warwickshire ring. Now our son Jamie and his wife Pam live a stone's throw from the canal side and we have a plan that when the grandchildren are older we shall take them barging up the cut and share with them the fun of it all.

Paul and I are keen bargers; we've been doing it for twenty years, and every Easter have taken two boats and about sixteen teenagers with us for the week.

Sometimes I think it may have been easier the other way round – two teenagers and sixteen boats – but – *hey ho!* – hindsight is a wonderful thing.

One of our butty stops today was beside the canal en route to Rugby. We had intended to stop at the pub for a coffee but it was shut due to refurbishments. Never mind; we sat and ate our butties by the canal side and I took a photo of Paul staring dreamily into the distance reliving fond memories.

I was beginning to have hope that one day I would do that about this bike ride.

Arriving early as we did meant that we had more time to play with our youngest grandson, Joseph, as well. Pam had told both the boys that we were on our way and every time Joseph saw a bike that day he said to Pam,

"Is that Granny and Grandad?"

When we did arrive, however, he was a little wary to begin with. He's two-and-a-half and not used to seeing Granny and Grandad dressed funny and with hats on, but he recognized us after our shower and everything was once again alright in his little world.

Up to this point we had been putting cream on our ever aching behinds in the morning before the ride, and sometimes at a toilet stop en route. Today was the first day we started applying it after the evening shower and before bed too; fortunately, we had a new pot waiting for us at the halfway mark at our home in Bosley.

My daughter-in-law Pam is a wonderful Irish girl. She under-stands me in a way that sometimes my husband doesn't; she recognized what a feat it had been for me to even get on the bike in the first place let alone ride up the country. And while Paul was collecting Daniel from school she presented me with my award.

Three family-sized packets of Minstrels and Malteasers.

Pam, you have a place in my heart forever.

She and I polished off one packet immediately and then ate the other two surreptitiously throughout the evening – and Paul never knew… until I read this paragraph to him just now.

We took photos of the boys on the tandem. It was very sweet as their feet didn't even touch the pedals and Joseph had to be held in place by Jamie. After we left Rugby the boys threw themselves into cycling and have both come on brilliantly. I have high hopes; give them a few years and they might take the tandem off our hands.

Pam served up a full beef roast dinner just as Paul likes it, along with Smartie ice cream and meringue for dessert, all washed down with buckets of red wine. She and I then settled on the sofa for the evening surrounded by a few hundred Malteasers, whilst Paul spent the time in the kitchen catching up with our son Jamie.

As I hauled myself up the stairs to bed that night, I did wonder if I would actually fit into my cycling gear in the morning. How embarrassing if we had to call the tour off due to weight gain!

My last thought as I hit the pillow was, "This has been a great day on the bike. It's so easy!" I knew those words would undoubtedly come back to bite me on my very sore bottom in a few days, but it really had been a great (part) day's cycling.

Comments / Texts

Morning, Paul & Annie, our love & prayers go with you on this new morning. It is very sunny here, hope the weather and hills are kind heading towards Rugby xx Read Colossians 1:29: "For this I toil struggling with all his energy that he powerfully works within me."

Jude

Arrived safe and happy around 2pm!
Yep! A great day. In bath already.
Looking forward to evening with grandkids.

Annie (to Super 7)

Sleep tight and may your bottom be restored to new life, sending many 100-mile-an-hour kisses.
xxxxxxxxxxxxxxxxxxxxxxxxxxxxxxxxxxxxxxxxxxxxxx

Maz

22ND MAY, 2014

STAGE 8

Rugby to
Barton-under-Needwood

Rain, rain, stay away!

...And it did!

It seemed to rain all around us, but not *on* us!

To be honest, God knows what I am like on a tandem in the rain, and, out of sympathy with Paul, kept it away.

After such a lovely stopover with our family I was a little reluctant to leave this morning and Paul had to drag me out of my comfy bed on his return from walking Daniel back to school. (He's an inspiration to grandads everywhere!) But John O'

Groats was still calling and so at 10am, a little later than usual, we set off for Barton-under-Needwood, via Hinkley, No Man's Heath, Clifton Campville, Coton in the Elms, and Walton-on-Trent. We only had forty-two miles to cycle today so leaving late was a happy circumstance.

The morning passed without incident, and we stopped for lunch at Stoke Golding.

The sign read, "The birthplace of the Tudor dynasty."

Now, I love anything to do with Tudor history, having read several books by historians on the subject. Heck, I even have the complete video box set of The Tudors, starring Jonathan Rhys Meyers – not that he bears any resemblance to King Henry 8th, or the series to actual history, but it is still my favourite summer holiday viewing. Even so, I couldn't figure how Stoke Golding held a significant place in Tudor history, until we saw signs for Bosworth nearby and then I obviously joined the dots between where we stood now and the famous battle between Richard III and Henry Tudor.

A more modern translation of, "A horse, a horse, my kingdom for a horse," could possibly be, "A car, a car, my tandem for a car."

I think Shakespeare would understand.

I wrote in our blog that night, "A prize to anyone who can put me right – you'll win the ride of your life!... on a tandem!... up to Scotland!"

There were no takers.

The butty stop at Stoke Golding was memorable for another reason too. Paul spied out what he thought was a pleasant looking park with a bench near the entrance, so we dismounted and set about lunch. I had nothing but food on my mind at this point and so grabbed the sandwiches and sat down whilst Paul gave the bike a bit of a once over. With a mouthful of jam and bread I glanced up to see an open grave in front of me. We had inadvertently decided to dine with the quieter residents in Stoke Golding cemetery. We both had to duck behind a bush to re-cream our nether regions but at least these neighbours wouldn't be complaining. We had each developed 'tender spots' on our derrière and the cream we use has an antiseptic property so kept blisters and such like at bay.

It also contains a mild anaesthetic, apparently.

Yeah, right. That's today's smile.

I took the opportunity to phone my friend Jude. She is married to Ian, and I had already sent her a text commiserating with her about that. Jude is my garden guru – what she doesn't know about gardening probably isn't worth knowing – and as I chatted with her about the weeds that were having their heyday in my garden in my absence, she volunteered to come round when we got home in June to do some clearing up with me. This is a woman who is busy, busy, busy, and yet happily offered to put time aside for me.

This is my friend.

My other friend (I have at least two), Derek the trucker, phoned shortly after and we had our usual daily catch up. He is always very encouraging and cheery to talk to, with boundless energy. I describe him as Tigger next to Ian's Eeyore type character. For the purposes of the tour, though, I began to refer to him as Mr

Motivator; I never thought of a name that summed up Ian's 'help' to me on the tour. Derek and I did discuss who would play whom in the Hollywood film version of our tour. I would selflessly play myself with Hugh Jackman in the lead as Paul, Vigo Mortensen would play Derek and after much thought we decided upon Victor Meldrew as Ian.

Despite the pleasant countryside, the afternoon was a struggle after such a delightful morning. It's always the same when we are nearing our destination; it seems as though the last five miles are longer than the first forty. We had no hiccups though apart from one when Paul braked suddenly and I flew forward off the saddle and straight into my handle bars.

"*Ouch,* darling! That hurt just a tinsy bit. Would you mind awfully warning me in future?" is the gist of what I said.

We arrived just after 2pm to a very warm welcome and cup of tea from Wendy and David, who seemed genuinely pleased to see us. It never ceased to amaze me how all our hosts, most of whom we didn't know, threw themselves into the part of providing a haven for us each night, treating us like celebrities, and were in some cases more excited about our journey than we were. To be fair, that wasn't very difficult in my case, but Paul was hard to compete with such was his enthusiasm.

We hit it off straightaway with David and Wendy and their dog Cara, and were treated to a wonderful meal of Gammon, cherry pie and custard. At this rate I may be the first person in history to actually put weight on whilst cycling LEJOG but, hey, I couldn't refuse, could I?

Our hosts had arranged for a few friends to meet with us for the evening, and John and John (every church must have at least one) came over and we spent a very enjoyable evening together. My usually reserved husband was positively wired with adrenaline on this adventure and threw himself into conversation like a man possessed.

We all trooped out to the back garden to have our photo taken complete with tandem for the local newspaper, and I offered money to anyone who would like to keep the blessed thing.

They all laughed heartily. They thought I was joking.

We fell into bed happy, knowing that we were being supported by old friends and new, encouraging us up the country with their love and prayers.

Comments / Texts

Sumtimes rain is a blessing so u don't get 2 hot hun! When I cycled the Coast 2 Coast I kept a flannel tucked down my cycling shorts (!) and doused it with sum cold water from my water bottle 2 wipe my face when required. It saved me on those uphills!
That's my tip 4 the day 4 U. Sending enormous hugs and kisses full of red bull and lucozade bottles of love!
U R doing amazing!

Maz

Hope u both slept well and managed a lie in. Lovely to c u. Safe onwards travel. Our thoughts and prayers go with u. Very proud of u. U can do it – keep those wheels rolling. x

Jamie

Morning, you two intrepid explorers. It's looking a bit like rain today so best put your lights on. I've been driving through some dreadful fog and spray so that one couldn't see a thing yet there are the braindead numpties with no illumination on them, must think we've all been to Specsavers. So please remember to be seen and safe, rather than in heaven with BMW printed on your bottoms.
Praying really hard for you today. God bless.

Ian

Hi, Annie and Paul. Just wanted to say hi and how fantastic you both are and how proud I am to call you both friends. Keep up the fantastic work.
Lots of love, hugs and prayers. x

Lesley

Hope the day is going well n rain holding off. Lovely to have you stay. V proud and impressed. Praying with u all the way. Just about to get in car and Joseph said, "Let's go find grandad's bike!"

Pam

Were just north of Hinckley eating our butties if u want to come find us!

Annie

Insistent as he is...
we need to go to Sainsbury's instead!

Pam

Arrived safe, good day, bottom hurts,
just about to have a bath. xx
Blog later.

Annie (to Super 7)

You're finishing earlier and earlier!

Simon

Stoke Golding – where Henry VII was crowned after the Battle of Bosworth. Very cool!

Hannah

You are right – the crown passed from Richard to Henry, but if you don't mind, thank you, I think I'll settle for the second prize – a week's labour down a salt mine – it will be a whole lot easier! Enjoy your rest tonight.

xxxxxxx

Thinking of you and so glad we saw you. Good luck.

Sheila

What a wonderful privilege it is for you both to be meeting, for a moment in your lives, these lovely hosts – God will, I am in no doubt, use this experience so productively. You have got to write up a living journal from this Tandem Tour. A few days ago, I was concerned about the sheer scale of what you had taken on and now I am not sure if you will want to stop when you reach your destination! You were very much the focus of the prayer group last night, guys. You will love Barton-under-Needwood, it's just up the road from my sister in Whittington.

Jude

Hi there – what interesting reading. You are such a plucky couple and we are full of admiration of you! We are not long back from holiday, hence our silence! Looking forward to meeting you soon.
Best wishes as you continue North.

Chris and Barry (future hosts)

We plan on coming to Bosley tomorrow... We can't let you be so close by without saying hello and "well done" personally!! The photos and blogs are brilliant and we are all journeying with you (sort of!) You keep moving and we will keep praying. The joy of seeing your family and friends, old and new, must be a great encouragement to you both.

John and Margaret

Well, Daniel told his supply teacher you were cycling to Scotland today... he will be upset by your lack of progress! Joseph however was still "looking for grandad's bike" at tea time... you are really confusing your grandchildren.

Pam

It's been great reading your updates and fantastic that things are going so well now.
We hope you have a great time tomorrow and enjoy your own bed tomorrow night!

Geoff and Claire

23RD MAY, 2014

STAGE 9

Barton-under-Needwood
to Bosley

Bosley! O Bosley! O beautiful Bosley!

Oh my goodness! I was rudely awakened by Paul's alarm at 6am which is still the middle of the night in my book. Paul had decided that if we left "super early", we would get to Bosley "super early" and enjoy an afternoon pottering at home. We also needed to get to Bosley St Mary Primary School this side of half-term so knew we had to get a wriggle on.

With breakfast under our belts – or cycling shorts, in our case – we were away at 8am. I don't think I've ever cycled at 8am; my legs are usually still in the prone position.

David said it was a privilege to meet us and we both felt incredibly humbled by this lovely man and his wife Wendy who had given us so much. We set off in happy mood; we were on our way to our own house for the night, where I was planning to superglue myself to the bed.

We made good progress and avoided all the rain showers; everything was hunky dory in my world.

And then we hit the A50.

We joined it at Utoxeter and stayed on it for a frightening half hour till Meir. It has to rank in the top three of my all time terror-filled moments, and I sobbed and wailed very loudly to make sure Paul could hear me above the traffic.

Most traffic gives generous room for bikes but some cars and lorries decide not to, for whatever reason, and the wind draft they create as they go by astonishingly close causes even more problems. I could have reached out and touched somebody's lorry a number of times.

Paul heard the weeping and wailing and gnashing of teeth and so put a sprint on to get us off the 'death dual' a.s.a.p. He reached back several times to touch my hand and shouted that all was OK, which did nothing to alleviate my fears as he was clearly off with the fairies somewhere and unaware of our present reality.

Eventually we got off the road from hell, and grumpily and bumpily cycled through to Meir town centre for the unhappiest of butty stops ever recorded. I was furious with Paul that he should plan such a dangerous route, and went very, very, quiet, which is worse than screaming. I think I was still in shock. By this time, we had cycled for twenty-eight miles without a break and I am used to coffee and cake at twenty. We both hit a sugar low and sat there, in silence, in the now pouring rain, devouring our increasingly soggy sandwiches.

There was one of those toilet cubicles on the pavement nearby that looks a bit like a grey Tardis, and I approached with caution. I have had bad experiences with these things in the past; not shutting properly, and opening at just the wrong time to reveal me in all my glory. However, I was desperate and the only other option was doing a Paula Radcliffe by the kerb.

The blessed thing was out of order. *Urrgghh!* (I was cross with Paul about *that* too.)

Tired, emotionally wrought and with bladder bursting, we cycled through Meir until we found a small wood on the outskirts and both spent some individual 'me-time' behind a tree. An empty bladder does help to lighten the mood and we sort of smiled at each other afterwards, but still didn't speak.

We made our way through Cheddleton and up to Wetley rocks where we stopped for a Costa coffee – the best! – and a Kitkat at the petrol station there.

I sat on the wall and told Paul as calmly as I could that I would have to kill him if he ever took us on another dual carriageway. I saw by the way he gulped a swallow that he had something to tell me about the rest of our journey.

He decided it was best not to share it with me at that moment, and I decided it was best not to ask.

A truck driver parked up and whilst Paul got the coffees I chatted with him, thinking to myself that his was probably one of the lorries that had darn near killed us an hour or so previously. I explained we were cycling Land's End to John O' Groats and he remained singularly unimpressed.

He was definitely one of the lorries, I thought.

With coffee and chocolate sloshing inside, my mood brightened, which meant Paul felt safe to venture conversation once more and we continued our journey towards Leek. We know this neck of the woods well, having cycled or motored through this area many times, and as we passed various landmarks it was like welcoming old friends.

A sign read "Leek, Queen of the moorlands" and since Paul was wearing his "King of the mountains" shirt, it seemed appropriate to stop and take a photo of the two of them together. By this time all terror was forgotten and we were friends once more, excitedly chatting to each other as we rode into town.

I phoned my friend Alec who had set up the opportunity for us to call in at the primary school in Bosley – being a governor there – and he was duly impressed that we were so near. It was twelve noon and we knew we would be there in the next half hour. Coming up out of Leek we saw our first glimpse of Bosley Cloud, the local small mountain and beauty spot. My heart truly did miss a beat; I knew we were within spitting distance of our home.

Right on cue, we got to Bosley St Mary at 12.30pm. I jumped off the bike and threw myself into Alec's arms. He must have thought, "Gosh, she's jolly glad to see me!"

I was – but in truth I was just jolly glad to be alive.

We had arrived at the perfect time, *lunch time*. The sun had chased the rain away, and all the children were playing outside. When they saw us, they descended upon us like a swarm, but a very nice swarm, and chatted and asked questions and then just as quickly lost interest and went back to playing in their friendship groups. Our fifteen minutes of fame lasted exactly that.

From the school it's a five-minute ride to our house. We live on a park home site in a wooden lodge that looks as though it would be right at home in the Swiss mountains. The private lane rises more than one hundred feet in less than half a mile, but it was a mere bump in the road to us; adrenaline and the thought of seeing friends and neighbours kept the wheels turning, we rounded the corner and there it was: our home.

We have some good friends on the site where we live and even before a bath I popped over to see Kathleen and Hughie. They had been collecting our post for us and were delighted to see us safe and well.

Whilst Paul gave the bike a complete overhaul and put the two new (tractor!) tyres on, I relished walking round the garden checking on all my plants. I had been looking forward to this; saying goodbye to some as their season was coming to an end and hello to others that were just making their entrance into this year's summer. We live at just over seven hundred feet above sea level, whereas Congleton just five miles down the road where our home church is situated is around two hundred. Because of that my garden is a late bloomer.

I know how it feels.

The whole garden was bursting with colour now; the Rhododendrons had never seemed so vivid, the peonies were out in all their splendour, some of the tulips were still swaying gently in the wind. It was a precious moment for me indeed. The weeds were having a party too, but never fear, Jude was on their case, their days were numbered.

After that I visited two other friends on site, Janette and Geoff. They are both keen cyclists and Janette was toying with the idea of doing LEJOG herself next year but wasn't sure she could do it.

"You are four stone lighter than me, you are super fit on the bike, you will eat the miles up... but beware Cornwall," was my answer.

After spending over a week in just cycling gear I couldn't decide what on earth to wear that night; there was just too much choice, and, believe it or not, I got a little stressed over it. We were going out for a meal with friends and I wanted to look my best but everything was just a little tight. I got on the bathroom scales which turned out to be a bad idea and quickly beat a hasty retreat to the bedroom where I had to lie down. I put all our cycling gear in the wash and then once more got lost in the garden; it was good to do what normal people do for a change.

Charlotte and our grandchildren Pippa and Jack picked us up in their car (ours was still in Exeter with my sister at that point). The children weren't overly impressed with our journey to date but, to be fair, it doesn't look that far on a map to a child of five. Our Jack had gotten some street cred out of our expedition though. One day at school in 'show and tell' he had taken our flyer with him and told his class all about it, though he did get a few facts wrong:

"They are cycling three hundred miles." Yes – and the rest, Jack!

His teacher had got the class to follow us on our blog after that.

Alec and his wife Ruth along with friends from Bosley, Trinity and Wellspring churches had laid on a feast for us. Many were already there when we arrived and we embraced them all. Most had been following our blog but it was still fun to add more to the stories and we laughed a great deal with the A50 consigned evermore to history. Dear friends from the charity Christian Relief Uganda who we were supporting were also there. It was like a massive emotional fuel injection – just what we needed – and we thanked God for every person, every friendship. Beef or chicken stew, rice, potatoes, peas and all manner of desserts awaited us.

I always feel a sense of duty in times like this to try absolutely everything so as not to offend anyone.

So I did.

Our friend Jason made a video of us to put on the blog so people could see us at the halfway mark. We had spent less than four hours in the saddle that day but had cycled forty-nine miles – 442 over all.

Bed was delightful, and if we had had the energy it could have been even more so but we pretty much conked out as soon as we climbed in.

Paul and I both knew it would need divine intervention to get me to leave home the next day.

Comments / Texts

Arrived at 1pm! (Left at 8am.) Sorry didn't text earlier, was in bath and then in garden.

Annie (to Super 7)

I don't like the A50 in a car let alone on a bike! You are two special people who it was a pleasure to meet. Mind how you go!

John

Wow – my hair is standing on end. I can remember what bike riding ear to ear with a lorry is like from my young days when there wasn't so much traffic. The back of a lorry comes dead level with the side of your head – and we never thought of riding with helmets then! You have now turned an 'elbow' on your journey – half-way up England... Hope you've got your rain-capes for today! That funny noise in your ears is me singing your song for you: "One more pedal..."

Mum

It was great to see you at Bosley Methodist earlier and to be able to confirm for ourselves that you are still in one piece (well two really!) after your journey so far. Sorry about the dual carriageway – perhaps in the remoter parts of Scotland there won't be many of those sorts of road!

Reading about Paul giving the bike a full service brought another 'bikers' worship song to mind:

"Give me oil on my gears, keep me cycling,
give me oil on my gears I pray,
give me oil on my gears, keep me cycling,
keep me cycling till we find the way."

The original version also mentions
joy in my heart – keep me singing,
and peace in my heart – keep me resting.

On your tour these seem very appropriate ideas! Please be encouraged as you set out once more, we suspect the Wellspring website and viewing of your blog is on serious overload at present! Have you thought of publishing a book of photos and daily experiences similar to the blog when you return from your adventure? It would be a shame to lose all this in the mists of time!

John and Margaret

I hadn't thought of it up 'til that point...

Is that Wetley rocks I see in the blog photo?
You were so close by, I'd have put some flashing lights
on the car and escorted you on the A50. Sorry that
your journey was so scary, Stoke isn't that bad really.
OK, well, maybe the A50 is a little crazy, I drive it daily.
I bet being home is the best feeling ever. You're
making great progress, you should be so proud.

Natalie

Thanks to all at Bosley Methodist for your hospitality!
The food was delicious and it was great to catch up
with "Granny and Grandad" too. Can't believe how
much we ate. Paul & Annie were the only ones who
had a good excuse to have 'seconds'! Plenty of energy
for Bosley to John O' Groats!

Simon

24TH MAY, 2014

STAGE 10

Bosley to Rainford

"Laughter in the rain"…?

Neil Sedaka clearly wasn't sat on a tandem going through Warrington in the rain when he wrote that song.

There were two halves to this day…

In the morning we had a relaxed start, having spent a wonderful evening of laughter and food with friends and family at Bosley Methodist, though I was unable to persuade anyone to take my place, so that was a little disappointing.

Bed was glorious! We had a new one, bought just a few weeks previously. It's one of those new fandangled things that you can lift up at one end and store stuff in; I thought about jumping in and hiding there so that Paul might go on without me.

He was an eager beaver waking us up for breakfast at 7, though completely adamant we wouldn't leave before 10. I assumed it was out of love for me; and in a roundabout way it was. He had secretly arranged for our son Simon and grandchildren to meet us in a lay-by near Knutsford at 11am; he knew it would be a lovely surprise for me.

I sat curled up on the sofa in my dressing gown reading the morning paper and refused to get ready:

"Bike ride? What bike ride?"

Before we left we knocked on the neighbours' doors so that they could wave us off, intrepid explorers that we were. They stood guarding our front door like bouncers so that I couldn't get back in even if I tried.

We took the back roads that we know so well to Knutsford and I sensed the enormity of leaving home and heading to Scotland… in my bladder… so we had to have a toilet stop at the side of a main road somewhere just beyond the town. There were a few trees lining the route and they shielded me from all but the most prying of eyes. By now I was getting used to bearing my bottom before the world though, and needs must.

We had cycled about twenty miles when Paul suggested we had our first butty stop in a lay-by "up yonder". I could see some children waving in the distance and thought, "How sweet!" Children do often stare and wave at us as we cycle by and people do smile; it's nice to provoke that reaction in people and I always enjoy smiling and waving back. Sometimes we've had people singing, "Daisy, Daisy," as we've ridden past which is a lot nicer than the usual greeting ("She's not pedalling..." – *that* one!)

I did think these particular children had jolly good eyesight though, to see it was a tandem from that distance. It was only when we were much nearer that I realized it was our Pippa and Jack. I was thrilled that Simon and Paul had concocted this to surprise me in such a delightful way.

As we approached I heard them call out,

"Come on, Granny, we want to see you pedal!"

So not funny.

Obviously coached by my very rude son.

I was clearly pedalling my heart out at the time to reach them.

I *was*.

We enjoyed a lovely half hour with the children and Simon, and I ate his crisps as a reprimand.

We left them reluctantly and headed round the corner into a few spots of rain; nothing we couldn't handle. Up to press it had been a good day, all hour-and-a-half of it, but that was about to change.

These little spots of rain brought their friends along and before we knew it we were in a deluge that stayed with us.

For thirty miles.

That wasn't funny either.

No laughter.

I suppose it could have been worse; we could have been on the A50.

We navigated our way through Warrington, crossing the river Mersey twice, so I had Gerry and the Pacemakers in my head for ages till we stopped for another butty by a huge roundabout on the outskirts.

This was not a happy time in my life. Paul has this great ability to make the best of any situation and he was chipper and upbeat and genuinely enjoying himself – and I wanted to punch him. He suggested that we record this happy occasion for posterity with a photograph; in his photo he is smiling with a glint of joy in his eye and a look that says, "I'm on this big adventure and I love it."

And then there is my photo.

MI6 are in talks with me about using it for interrogation purposes.

We still had fifteen miles to go and it hadn't given up raining. I'm sure that for many reading this, fifteen miles is no hard thing, but like mogwais I turn into a gremlin when cycling and rain come together; add hills to the mix and you have the perfect recipe for a very unhappy Annie. Despite his joie-de-vie, Paul must have felt just a little nervous with this ticking time-bomb sat behind him, twelve inches from his nether regions.

A chap on the pavement called out the usual greeting:

"She's not pedalling at the back, you know..."

Oh, here we go… It would have been funny if I wasn't wet, cold, tired, and fed-up.

I smiled, but not on the inside.

An eternity later we arrived at Marylyn and Bill's. I tried hard not to cry but the tears came and no one noticed through the rivers of rain and my hair plastered to my face. We suggested to Bill that walking through their front door might cause a flash flood in their hallway so we used the tradesman entrance via the garage and brought our very own pond with us as we dripped all over the floor.

Bill and Marylyn are absolutely delightful funny people but at this moment they must have wondered what on earth they had let themselves in for. Neither Paul nor I were really responding to Bill's gentle wit. For myself I think I was in a trance. Paul was all business-like; get the bike sorted, get our bag of bits offloaded, and him straight in the shower.

I attempted to make conversation, having been given a huge cup of tea, but I couldn't think of a single positive thing to say, and to this day cannot remember much at all about that moment, other than sitting on their stool with an extremely loud squelch and muttering, "It's been horrible," over and over.

Bath-time was delightful and I took my time; I needed space. I could hear laughter from downstairs somewhere and knew Paul was settled well and would cope without me for a while longer. Usually I want to be where all the action is, but not this time; I enjoyed my very own private little meltdown in a tub of hot water.

I was a different woman when I ventured into the living room. The four of us got on brilliantly and we spent a great evening sharing together about family, faith, and life experiences in serious and humorous conversation over another superb meal. We did our nightly routine of me writing the blog, both of us choosing the pictures to accompany it, and Paul doing all the techy stuff to get it sent out.

We went to bed around 8pm and I decided to look over the texts we had received that day. Ian had sent some particularly hilarious ones in this first part of the tour that I hadn't fully appreciated at the time so we snuggled up in bed and read everything he had sent and howled with laughter.

It was more a case of laughter *after* the rain.

Comments / Texts

You will be over half way soon, and back home before u know it!! Thinking of you today. xxx

Pam

Hi you two! We're leaving around 10am if you want to come and take our place... whoops, I meant wave us off!

Annie (to neighbours Geoff and Janette)

Morning both. Hope it wasn't too much of a wrench leaving home this morning (you have gone, haven't you?) After hearing your story last night of Paul the great cycle god I have no fear that you are well on the way. I woke this morning with an image of Paul like a great Olympiad striding down the path; chest out and shoulders back with the bike in one hand and a fist full of your hair in the other, calling out to the world:
"Come on, woman, the adventure awaits!"
Now that's the way to treat your wife!
Bless you both and God speed.

Ian

...another night, another guest bed...

Annie (to Charlotte)

Have arrived after a lot of rain and traffic,
another 49 miles, I think we're just over halfway now.

Annie (to Super 7)

Wow! Brill! Awful weather!

Pat

I was so not a happy bunny!
Hope it's not like this tomorrow.
I'm so thankful we're just doing 50 miles a day.
I couldn't cope with longer. My bottom is SO sore.

Annie

Mmm, sure it must be!! Have a relaxing bath now. xx

Pat

Glad yr safely there. Well done on hitting the halfway
mark – less to come than has already gone!

Jamie

So glad! Today was hard work coz of the rain,
it really takes the joy away.

Annie

...joy?...

Jamie

Lovely video. So enjoyed seeing you both in such great
heart and spirit. Bless you – just... 'keep on pedalling'
the way you do... from one county to the new...

Mum

So good to have seen you 'in real life' last night to share big hugs. Bosley certainly did you proud. Lovely photos and video message to encourage us that you are still very positive and for us to ensure through prayer that you remain that way for the next 11 days! Ian says: "Paul, that is not a giant hamster you have woken up next to this morning, it is just Annie storing cake from last night!" – how rude!
Love you lots.

Jude

Hello you two! I am trying (very trying some would say!) to send you a message, so good to see you last night, what a lovely evening, wonderful food and hospitality from Bosley Church. Hope the weather is better tomorrow, sending lots of prayers and love. xxx

Sue

Thinking of you both now the rain has returned, keep going! Your blog, pictures and video are so interesting and inspirational. As someone who has embraced the joys of cycling in my 50s and knowing the enormous amount of sheer determination and God-given strength that you need on occasion, I think what you are doing is BRILLIANT!!

Bev and Andy

25ᵀᴴ MAY, 2014

STAGE 11

Rainford to Carnforth

Easy peasy, lemon squeezy

We had fifty-four miles ahead of us on this day and I sincerely hoped the weather was going to be better than on the previous one. Our cycling clothes had been hung near radiators around the kitchen and were nice and dry and ready for wear, not that we paraded naked into the kitchen to get them. (What happens at home stays at home!) We each had a complete second cycling outfit to wear, so came to breakfast suitably attired.

I had had a dreadful nightmare during the night — something about cycling the length of Britain — just to wake up and discover it was true.

Often a bad or emotional dream can set the tone of the day for me but I knew breakfast with Marylyn and Bill would lift my spirits – and it did. They really are a comedy act; Marylyn plays it more straight as a foil to Bill's funny man routine. We laughed throughout and then had the privilege of praying for them, and them for us, before we left at nearly half past nine.

It was Sunday morning so we sang our hearts out to God as we rode along. Goodness knows what pedestrians thought, but we didn't mind and gave 'Thine Be the Glory' our best shot. The weather was improved, we had a hearty breakfast inside us, prayers over us and a day of not too hilly cycling in front of us, plus the added anticipation of knowing we would be Skyping our home church, Wellspring, later that morning and speaking with the fellowship live via the big screen.

We had only cycled for about an hour and a half when we had our first butty stop just off the main road somewhere south of Preston. We needed to eat and be ready to skype at 11am.

A horse in the field behind us joined in our selfie photo and then, bored by our chat and the lack of us wanting to share our well earned butties with him, wandered off to enjoy his own company once more.

We were like excited children as we prepared to contact Wellspring. I could not contain myself, bouncing around and getting very keyed up. When we did make contact, however, it was a case of "Wellspring, we have a problem" in that they could see and hear us but we couldn't hear them at all! Even so, our contact man there – Alan Rafferty – moved the camera slowly round the church giving us a great close up of his nostrils before it panned out and we could see everyone waving at us.

"Look! There's Catherine... and Kath, and... who's that? Oh yes! It's Jason."

On and on we went, identifying everybody, laughing and waving feverishly back oblivious to the fact that they wouldn't see the hand gestures as we held the phone far too close for comfort and they too were treated to close ups that only married couples should have to endure.

Despite the technical hitches it was a real thrill to see everyone and know that they hadn't secretly moved in our absence.

Our mood was soaring as we took off once more and navigated our way through Preston. I hate cycling through towns on the bike and the bigger the town the more I hate it, but we managed with the help of the GPS and stopped for a coffee at Garstang.

The threat of rain hovered over us throughout the day but it never actually happened, though I don't know that anything could have dampened our spirits that day; seeing our fellowship and knowing just how much they were supporting us with texts, blogs and prayers was uniquely inspiring.

We were always aware that people were thinking of us, wondering how we were getting on each day, waiting to hear from us. I know of several couples who spent the day mentally on the bike with us:

"Where did they start from this morning?... Oh, that's right... Let's look at the map... Right, they're probably about here at the moment... Golly! Look at those contours, that's going to be a hill and a half to climb when they get there... I wonder if Annie's pedalling at the back..."

Near Garstang we came across a pub called The Roebuck so clearly we had to stop for a photo call. A helpful gentleman was passing and took a couple of photos for us.

Whenever I hand my camera to someone I don't know I'm always a little worried that they will run off with it, and considering my Blackberry held so many pictures of our ride, plus all my diary notes, I was reassured to see that this particular member of Joe Public was not in prime condition or age, and therefore running after him wouldn't be too much of an ordeal.

For Paul.

We carried on our adventure and a cyclist went past us – always a humiliation in the cycling world – and called out the usual greeting; you know the one:

"She's not pedalling at the back."

If I got £1 for every time I have heard that, both charities we're supporting would be flush for years!

We took a cycle path that ran by the side of the beautiful Lune estuary. At one point we dismounted just to stop and enjoy the view – 'What is this ride if, full of miles, we have no time to stop and smile?' and all that.

We had a butty too which made it all the more worthwhile.

It was here that I received the most infamous text of all from my once-upon-a-time friend Ian. He had spent the day travelling down to Guildford by car and was tired:

"...even though like you, Annie, I'm just a passenger..."

Outrageous.

Utterly outrageous.

Whilst Paul choked with laughter on his butty, I texted straight back,

"I AM NOT JUST A PASSENGER!"

I reckoned Ian's wife Jude knew nothing of the sort of things he was writing and I vowed to show her all his texts when we got home. Then he would surely suffer. Oh yes, that would put him in the doghouse for at least three weeks.

Speaking of dogs, we met a couple who were walking their owners as we cycled along. The path was quite narrow at this point and even though the dogs were only small we decided to dismount to let the little group pass.

The humans were an elderly couple and we quickly got into conversation with them. I told them of our journey and they were duly impressed, and rightly so, I felt. I needed that after Ian's atrocious remark. Their dogs were called Bracken and Robby but I have no idea what the couple were called. Isn't it strange how we can ask the name of the pet, but it seems intrusive to ask the name of the owner?

Odd that.

As we headed for Lancaster I felt my stomach ball into a fist again at the thought of another huge town with lots of cars, but we were pleasantly surprised; Lancaster is beautiful and delightfully easy to navigate through. We had to stop several times in order for me to take photos of the castle up on the hill. Maybe because it was a Sunday it wasn't so busy, I don't know, but it was a joy cycling through this historic town. It also heralded the fact that we were not too far from our destination.

We reached Carnforth and the home of Julie and Ken at 3pm.

I had met Julie and Ken at the back end of last year at a disco. They were sitting with Jude and Ian, and as I wandered over, Jude introduced us and spoke of our plans to cycle the length of Britain.

Julie, bless her, piped up, "If you come anywhere near us, we'll put you up!" and we swapped numbers

Now was time to collect.

They didn't answer their front door.

We had cycled fifty-four miles in just under four-and-a-half hours. We needed rest. We knocked again.

No answer.

We telephoned.

Just then we saw the curtain twitch and assumed they were hiding behind the sofa, and so we were relentless in knocking and phoning until they had to give up and let us in.

"We were in the back garden. We didn't expect you for at least another hour!"

The curtain twitcher was the cat.

Phew!

One shower, several cups of tea, two glasses of red and a three course meal that would fit well in any first class restaurant, and I was buzzing!

We were so fortunate in that all our hosts had been charming people with a sense of humour and each evening an absolute tonic to the trials of whatever the day had been. Julie and Ken were no exception to the rule and we spent a very pleasant evening in their company.

Ken is quite a cyclist too, it turned out; more of a cyclist than me at any rate, and he and Paul shared information, suggestions, stories and such, like strangers who meet at a Star Trek convention.

We discovered that Ken had another hobby too; he led us to their third bedroom with growing excitement and gesticulations to see his pride and joy: a model railway system complete with train station, several lines, trains, bushes and trees, embankments, scenery and figurines all to scale.

Magnificent.

The whole track lined two walls and under the layout was what seemed like hundreds of wires going here, there and everywhere with switches, lights and buttons. All the above table tracks were represented beneath in a purpose-built diagram and Ken knew exactly what to press, flip or whatever to get the signal lights to work, the trains to move and switch lines.

It was an incredible piece of electrical wizardry and imagination. It was fascinating to witness how caught up Ken was with this miniature wonderland and I appreciated how hard he had worked and how fastidiously in order to make it as lifelike as possible.

The closest we had got to showing people the reality of our journey was a 3ft map of Britain with dots to mark our daily destinations and a big moveable yellow arrow stating "We are here" that I had set up in the church foyer before we left. I had thought it was jolly good at the time but now it seemed somewhat basic in comparison.

We retired to bed at 8pm, tired but happy. There I discovered on their shelves a book, Cat Haiku, which was a lot of fun to read, and clearly the writer knew her subjects.

Haiku is a Japanese form of prose that I was introduced to at Matt and Anna's wedding. (They are the young couple that I held responsible for our present predicament.) She is part American, part Japanese. It's an unusual type of verse: 3 lines, 5-7-5 syllables, rhyme not necessary.

For example:

> My biggest questions;
> Why am I on a tandem?
> Why did I do this?

And...

> My bottom is sore,
> The rest of me hurts as much.
> I am doomed. DOOMED. DOOMED!

I made up quite a few that night as I lay in the dark. I found it strangely comforting.

Comments / Texts

Hey! We couldn't hear the church but we saw you all and it was absolutely fantastic! God bless you lots.

Annie (to several people during morning service at church)

Just read your text out in church, we all send our love.

Catherine

It was gud 2 c u both this morning even tho conversation was 1 sided.
Am amazed at yr progres and gud spirits, our prayers r with u and those who r giving u b+b.
luv to u both.

Eileen and Alan

There's a simple solution to all these "passenger" remarks... Annie on the front and Dad at the back. Marriage is all about trust. Surely Dad trusts you enough to steer and brake (though you may be a little too keen on the brakes, Annie!)
Dare you to try it for just one day of your tour?

Simon

Arrived safe at Julie and Ken's in Carnforth.
Just had shower. Both perky today!

Annie (to Super 7)

Hopefully not too perky in someone else's house
or poor Charlotte won't cope!
Well done. U have inspired Joseph, he picked up his
balance bike and took off 20 mins ago, after screaming
every time he saw it for the last few months!

Pam

I'm so pleased it's going well; missing our coffees at the
garden centre, we will have to go at about 8am when
you're back so we've enough time to catch up.

Pat

Hello Annie and Paul, thanks for this morning's call, it
was great to see you both. Everyone was thrilled. We
know why you couldn't hear us so sorted for future.
Try Ps 121 with change of emphasis in v1-2 for next 2
days! God bless you both.
Psalm 121:1-2 reads, "I lift my eyes up to the
mountains, where does my help come from? My help
comes from the Lord, maker of heaven and earth."

Philip and Pauline Owens

Hope you've arrived safely with less traumas than you had yesterday.
I think you may have arrived before we did as it took us 5 hours to drive down to Guilford.
I'm worn out, I can tell you, and I was just the passenger like you, Annie. Anyway we're thinking of you and praying for you. Blessings.

Ian

I AM NOT A PASSENGER!

Annie

PS. I'm not really a passenger when Jude is driving, I think I actually work harder than she does but don't tell her.

Ian

I am going to show Jude all the texts you have sent when we return and she will put you on the naughty step for 3 weeks. Consider it payback! Managed to Skype church this morning!! Lots of love. xx

Annie (not a passenger)

26TH MAY, 2014

STAGE 12

Carnforth to Langwathy

The hills are alive with the sound of a meltdown!

Our usual routine in place, Paul got up around 7am to shave, dress and prepare mentally for the day ahead. I got up a good deal later and lurched unsteadily on tired, aching bones down the stairs to breakfast with Ken and Julie.

With a good cup of tea to wake me up I began to join in the discussion. Ken and Julie were getting ready to have French people stay the following weekend and having lived in the French speaking part of Belgium for a year when I was a teenager, I decided to regale them with my horror stories of conversations going haywire through mistranslation.

The best (worst) is the one I will tell you now. Please note that I had 'Unclassified' for my 'O' level mark tucked under my belt when I ventured to Belgium in the first place.

I had joined Operation Mobilisation (a Christian youth evangelism organisation) as an eighteen-year-old and was posted with a group of young people I'd never met before to the French-speaking part of Belgium, to a town called Charleroi. Part of the organisation's ethos was to sell books about Christianity door-to-door (this was early 1980s). There I was with my Finnish friend Helena, who spoke great English but no French, on the doorstep, when a very pleasant man answered. It was raining, we were tired, he invited us in and we stupidly agreed.

I tried to tell him in pigeon-French about the books, when he came straight to the point:

"Voulez-vous faire l'amour?"

"Oi, oi," I whispered to Helena, "I think he's cracking on to us; if I'm not mistaken (I was!) he's just asked us if we're in love with anyone at the moment. Just nod and say yes and he'll leave us alone."

We both nodded vigorously.

"Maintenant?" he enquired.

I knew that word for sure; it meant 'now'.

We both nodded our little heads off.

He left the room for a few minutes, and to this day I do not want to think about what he was doing, but when he came back he asked the question once more:

"Voulez-vous faire l'amour?"

At that moment the very few French lessons I had ever paid attention to started to kick in and from the depths of my brain came a little question of my own.

"Hang on," I thought, "the verb for 'to be' is 'etre', or something like that, and he didn't say 'etre', he said 'faire'... What does that mean?"

Suddenly, in a moment of shocking clarity I realised what he had said. (My French teacher would be proud of me.)

Oh blow! He hadn't asked, "Are you in love?" He had asked, "Do you want to *make* love?"

Aaaggghhh!

Helena was still smiling and nodding for all her worth when I told her to, "Zip it and get the heck out of here!"

"C'est domage [it's a shame]," said the horrible, greasy little slime-ball – how could I not have noticed that before? – and then he added insult to injury by offering us the equivalent of £3 each if we stayed!

I told him what he could do with his £3 in words that probably span most European languages, and Helena and I ran down the road and spent the rest of the afternoon in a coffee shop, wavering between laughing uncontrollably and then staring gloomily into our coffee cups at the thought of what might have been.

Both Ken and Julie thought that question probably wouldn't come up in conversation next weekend.

Julie packed us up a fantastic butty lunch complete with a large slab of Kendal Mint Cake. She clearly recognized Paul and I were in the same league as Sir Edmund Hilary and Sherpa Tensing who took KMC up Everest with them, and like them we would be climbing our own Everest today up to Tebay and then Shap Fell.

We set off just gone 9am and took the route out of town that Ken suggested would be shorter; it wasn't but I still love you Ken.

Our first stop of the day was at a great little coffee shop in Kirkby Lonsdale, halfway up the main street on the left hand side (never forget it, just its name, unfortunately!) During our training months prior to LEJOG, Paul and I had brought our tandem to Horton-in-Ribblesdale for a week in February, and had cycled all around the area including Ingleton and Kirkby Lonsdale, so we knew this coffee shop well and they do really do the best coffee and cake in town.

From there it was onwards and upwards on the bike, but downwards in my head as I struggled more and more with the hills / mountains. We stopped halfway up Shap Fell for a wee and a butty, and the photo I took of Paul for the blog that night had the following caption underneath:

"Even heroes need a butty stop."

He had worked hard to keep my mental head above water.

The scenery was pretty spectacular though, which was some consolation.

Cycling atop Shap Fell we came across an Australian lady, Ann, who was walking – and lost. Paul rescued the damsel in distress by working out on his GPS where she was and where she needed to be; a 180 degree turn and five miles back the other way was all that was needed. (So glad I wasn't her!)

While Paul was busy with his gismo she and I fell into conversation about all things Australian, mainly Neighbours.

She didn't watch it.

I was visibly shocked.

I became progressively more tired and therefore tetchy as the day wore on, but Paul announced along with "not far to go now" that there were no more hills. That did my heart good until we got to Langwathby, within four miles of our night-time stop, when there in front of me was another hill the size of Mount Fuji.

I was absolutely furious with Paul. I felt he had put it there deliberately and I refused to cycle up it. Instead, I got off and stomped up the hillside which probably took far more energy than riding up on the tandem would have done. I can see that now, but Paul was wise to keep that little snippet of wisdom to himself at that point.

I can hear you all saying, "Poor Paul," but I don't think you appreciate just how hard it is for me pushing him up some of these mountains!

The thing is, Paul loves hills, he really does, I can't quite put the emotion into words. He will cycle out of his way to go up one just for the sheer fun of it. I feel passionately about them too. His enthusiasm and zest for all things hilly really does test our marriage at times.

As does mine, I guess.

We eventually arrived at Hazel and Peter's after a frenzied ride up and down their road with me in tears looking for their house.

It has a name, not a number.

Eat your heart out, Patrick McGoohan.

Peter and Hazel were warm and welcoming and a calming influence on me in particular. We chatted away and in conversation we quickly discovered that they were both professional counsellors. It was going to be a long night.

For them.

A warm house, good food and a drop of wine were all that was needed to send us to lullaby land and by 8pm we were shot; we bade our goodnights and headed for the bedroom, but before that we took two photos of Hazel and Peter; one looking chipper after counselling Paul, and one after talking with me – they looked wrecked.

Of course, it was all a set up...

Comments / Texts

Hi, hope it's going well today. Just thinking about Thursday & wondering if you'd like fish, salmon maybe, or prefer casserole or cottage pie?

Chris and Barrie

We love all 3! Lovely to hear from you, we feel like we already know you now.

Annie

Hi you – keep up the pedalling! Where are you now? So feel for you if you are in the wet and windy weather we are experiencing here. x x
Hang on in – you will win through. x

Sara

Sorry we've been out all day so I haven't had chance to phone. We prayed for you before the short thanksgiving service and what's more people actually came to it, praise God! Hope you're doing well, you must be in the lakes by now, not long till you're in beautiful Scotland. Keep going you two, you're amazing and we are all proud to be your friends. Love you very much. May God's blessing go with you keeping you positive when the going is tough.

Derek

Yo! My best mates Annie and Paul. Good to hear that Ken and Julie were hiding behind the furniture, a wise move if you ask me especially after reading yesterday's blog. Anyways up, sounds to me as if you'll be climbing again today, Shap isn't it? So it will be all power to the pedals but that won't be a problem with your newly honed thighs. Hope Paul realizes that with all these hills Brazil nuts won't be the only things you'll be able to crack. Still, we are praying for you with every turn of the wheel and hope to speak to you soon. Yours in Christ our Lord, love from Jude and the passenger.

PS. Jude says you need to keep on praying for me but I can't think why.

Ian

I can.
Have just climbed up the equivalent of Everest near Tebay but we're on the way to Scotland! Need to find a coffee shop soon, after all what is this tour all about?

Annie

Arrived nearly 2 hrs ago so busy talking forgot to text! All ok, will blog later. xx

Annie (to Super 7)

What are you complaining about, Annie? Stuart and I have been up Shap Fell dozens of times with hardly any effort at all – all right I admit we were always in a car while doing it. Try doing it that way next time.

Stuart and Janet

You're doing amazing. Keep pedalling.
I sat in a car all day today and I feel exhausted so goodness knows how you feel.

Natalie

...My dad used to bike to work. Attached to his bike he had a small petrol engine called a Vincent Firefly. You had to pedal to get the engine going and it then took you up hills without the need to pedal anymore. This could have been useful to you on the tandem, but perhaps it would be cheating. All is well here and under control, you just pedal and relax!
Hope the tea break stops are well placed; over the border there may be one or two distilleries handy to help with refreshment. "Drunk in charge of a tandem" might be a first.

John and Margaret

Hold onto that Von Trapp mindset and sing your way up and down those mountains that stand before you! And you are on the 'downhill' side of your epic tour with just a very small country yet to conquer. YOU CAN DO IT GUYS, we all believe in you both. Love and blessing.

Jude

I was up the ladder yesterday cutting the hedge and a man on a tandem passed by, I thought for a moment Paul had escaped! Keep going, this time next week it will all be done!

Sue

27ᵀᴴ MAY, 2014

STAGE 13

Langwathy to Eskdalemuir

"Och aye the noo" to you too!

We needed to be up early for breakfast and leave by 8.30am as Peter had to be in Carlisle for 10, so after my usual trip to the bathroom as nerves overtook my body again, we set off.

Today we were heading into truly unchartered territory: Scotland. We'd only been cycling a short while when we came through Kirkoswald, which I lovingly (?) renamed Kirk-hill-oswald for obvious reasons. 'The Only Way Is Up' by Yazz was set on replay in my head. Believe me, it was the most fitting of songs in that moment.

We rode through the beautiful Cumbrian landscape passing through Hazelgill, Cumrew towards bonny Scotland.

As we rode along in the sunshine we came across an unusual sight. From a distance it looked as though someone had pegged out all their black socks on the barbed wire at the edge of the field by the roadside. Closer inspection showed that they were moles. They weren't sunbathing; they were dead. Very.

Why on earth would someone peg up dead moles like that? There were twenty of them so clearly it wasn't as a deterrent to other naughty little diggers. They wouldn't understand that anyway. We have found out since that the 'mole catcher' employed by the farmer to catch the "cute, furry little creatures with every right to be there" / "horrid little blighters" (depending on your view) would peg them up to prove how many had been caught, for payment purposes.

I jumped off the bike to take a photo and nearly passed out with the smell.

As I have already stated, we often got comments from Joe Public as we cycled along and this day was the best yet. Actually there were four; all in the space of about fifty metres as we endeavoured to ride up yet one more hill in one more Cumbrian village.

"She's not pedalling at the back." Yes, ha ha, heard that one before, very funny...

"Can yer ride tandem?" Sometimes I really wish I couldn't.

"Well, the pedals are turning but the wheels aren't going round!" Everyone's a comedian in this village!

And then there was my all-time personal favourite:

"Where are you heading?" asked a little old man leaning on his garden gate.

Giddy with excitement at someone taking a personal interest I yelled back,

"John O' Groats!"

"Uganda?" he said.

I know. I don't understand it either.

On reaching Castle Carrock, the village sign read "Please dance" instead of the usual "Please slow down", so I got off once more and did a little grapevine to the left, kick-ball-cross, four pivots, and a grapevine back again.

I am a line-dancer, and not a closet one either, I am out and proud.

Several years ago when hoping to prevent a lap-dancing club opening in Macclesfield, I announced to the council,

"I'm a lap-dancer myself." I meant line-dancer; I was confused.

If I was a lap-dancer I would break someone's legs.

I am not the slip of a girl I once was.

Castle Carrock sounded Scottish and we knew we were close so I called out to a young woman pushing a pram:

"Are we in Scotland yet?"

"No, no. About fifteen miles to go!"

Scotland would have to wait a while longer then and we stopped at Brampton for a coffee. People notice a tandem far more than a single bike and I always felt like a minor celebrity as we rode through towns; it was all I could do to resist the urge to give a queenly wave as we peddled past pedestrians. Many people do wave and smile back and in that moment in time they join with us in our adventure.

We parked / moored – I don't know really, what do you do with a bike? – and Paul headed in to get our coffee and cake whilst I chatted with the locals. A chap named Paul (easy for me to remember) sat there with his dog Dave, and as we bantered he handed me a huge bar of Dairy Milk chocolate.

Oh, thank you, God!

He then told me to unwrap it and give it to Dave.

Everything in my head seized up. This was not the way it was meant to be. Surely that was a bad move for two reasons:

1. Should you really give a dog that much chocolate?

2. Should you really give a dog that much chocolate when I could eat it instead?

It was his dog and his Dairy Milk. Never have I been so upset to give chocolate away. The blinkin' dog 'woofed' it down (excuse the pun) without it even touching its taste buds.

A complete waste.

Philistine.

And then it was back to the hills. (If you, dear reader, are fed up with the hills, that will be a small indication to you of how I felt.)

At one point we were so slow heading up that when a rabbit ran ahead of the bike, for the life of us we couldn't catch it! It even stopped for elevenses and a mid-morning nap in the road and was still perfectly safe from our wheels.

My friend Janette, who is thinking of doing LEJOG herself (don't read this book then), blogged to ask what gradient the hills were. Because we were on the byways, not the highways, and were taking back lanes wherever possible, we ventured up some pretty steep climbs. One today had been 20% and that wasn't unusual.

What seemed an eternity later I called out to a man digging his garden,

"Are we in Scotland yet?"

"No, no, about three miles down the road."

Scotland was playing hide-and-seek.

"Are we in Scotland yet?"

"Just down the hill and over the bridge!"

I know it sounds odd but crossing into Scotland on the tandem with Paul has to be in the top ten of my greatest experiences. As we headed over the bridge at 12.36pm exactly, the sign read, "Welcome to Scotland!"

We whooped, we cried, we got off and took a selfie. Derek the trucker rang at that moment.

"We're in Scotland!" I yelled. "We're in Scotl…" and then the line went dead, but I think he got the message!

He and Ian had phoned every day to encourage us and it was special to share that moment with him of all people.

Now we had arrived in Scotland we knew we could make it to the end. It really was a special milestone. From here on in, even though there were tough days ahead, my mood began to change from "I can't do this" to "I have nearly done this", and together we began to live more in celebration mode than a day-to-day existence.

We mounted our trusty steed once more and I sang every Scottish song I could think of which at that moment was precisely three – 'O Flower of Scotland', 'Marie's Wedding' and 'The Skye Boat Song' – and then burst into tears and we had to stop again.

I took that moment to compose myself and text everyone this side of the Atlantic that we had indeed arrived in Scotland. As an uneducated English Sassenach I always thought Scotland was a little bit at the top of England; in actual fact we still had a week's pedalling to do.

My mobile bleeped all afternoon, "Message from the dark side there is," as one by one people responded with hoorays, well wishes, "Och I denew" (Derek), "Och the nooo" (Jude), "Hookah the noo" (Ian).

My sister and friend Pat didn't attempt the impossible and just sent "Whoopee" and "Woo Woo" respectively.

Our evening stop was to be at a B&B in Eskdalemuir paid for by Eskdalemuir Parish Church, and we were told they wouldn't be doing us an evening meal so we saved our butties from Hazel's kitchen and stopped in Langhome for a meal at another ubiquitous coffee shop.

Desperate for a toilet stop, I asked where the toilets were. A dour Scotswoman confided in serious tones,

"We don't let customers use the toilet, they block it up."

I was in two minds whether to say, "OK then, I'll piddle on your floor," or, "I promise I'll be good."

I plumped for the latter and vowed I would only do the absolute minimum necessary.

Having only had a cake and no chocolate at Brampton we were both ravenous and had a three-course meal each, which was a good thing, except that we still had about twenty miles to cycle. With bellies full and bladders empty – "Thank you so much for letting us use the toilet" – we tried to get on the bike. I did think the frame might collapse with the weight, or that my cycling trousers would burst their seams, but somehow we set off with soup, jacket potatoes, cake and several cups of coffee sloshing around inside us.

Hazel's butties were safe for a while yet.

On very full stomachs we cycled the final miles to Eskdalemuir and in that stretch of road came across more pot-holes than in the rest of our entire journey. As a rule, the roads became better the farther we travelled up the country, and so did the cycle paths, come to think of it, but this road was a nightmare. We discovered later that it was because of logging in the area and the very heavy truckloads travelling along the roads.

The sun shines on the righteous and we therefore enjoyed pleasant weather all day until six miles from our destination when the rain set in. I can only think that Paul must have had some naughty thoughts at this point so it was his fault.

Once we arrived in Eskdalemuir we stayed at the wonderful Watcarrick B&B, and when Jock the proprieter, cook, and chief bottle washer-upper heard that we were cycling LEJOG, he said that he always cooked for cyclists and would have done so had he known. He and Roz run the place and we can honestly recommend it to anyone and everyone. They were delightful, the place was delightful, and I could use the toilet to my heart's content.

Happy days.

Comments / Texts

Are we nearly there yet?

Ian

!?+*!?!

Annie

More expletives! Gosh, yesterday must have been a real killer. I read your blog in bed last night; it was much more exciting than John Wesley's journal although he did cover more ground in a day.
Not on a tandem though.
I had considered that yesterday was going to be a huge pull for you both which is why I texted what I had hoped was a very uplifting message (no pun intended). Sadly it didn't seem to be enough.
Still now you can look on the bright side as what goes up also comes down so let's pray that it's just the tandem and not your mood.
I'm not sure about the terrain anymore as I have not ventured over that part of the country so I wouldn't know if it's flat or not. But after yesterday I'm praying that it's not.
Not to worry and I'll speak to you later.
Keep smiling and enjoy the tea breaks.

Ian

Sorry, that should read – I'm praying that it IS flat. Before you totally un-friend me.

Ian

We're in SCOTLAND!

Annie

Yay! We're in WALES!

Helen

O dear! All the best!

Simon

Och the knooo (or however you spell it).
We are so proud of you. Get out your tartan togs
and cycle forth. Glad you are so H-A-P-P-Y.
Speak later, lots of love and thank you Lord.

Jude

Hookah the noo! So it's tatties and neeps with your
haggis for tea tonight before a wee dram to warm
the bed linen.

Ian

Well done you pair, Scotland! Sending you both a
warm and fuzzy cuddle.

Maz

Wahey! You've reached MacGregor land! Watch out for
those haggis in the hills, they'll have your ankles.

Natalie

Have arrived safe at Eskdalemuir. Good day, tired but very happy. So excited to be in Scotland.

Annie (to Super 7)

Welcome to the Promised Land.

Chris and Barry

Well done – SCOTLAND!! … You must be very elated! We didn't realize the border was so far down! Sorry, that's not very helpful, is it? Keep smiling and singing.

Geoff and Janette

Whoop whoop! You have made it… home straight now… although there may be few bends, and dare I say the 'h' word! Dinnae bae crabbit wae Paul!!!!!

Pam

Did you have your passports with you?

Catherine

I am REALLY impressed! And remember it's downhill all the way back…

Veda

Wow, I DO believe it…
Well done, am thrilled to see Scotland, perhaps not as thrilled as you two were…
Can't wait to read the Book!!

Rhona

I want to bring you an uplifting message... When you start to type "Annie and Paul" into Google, it comes up with "Annie and Paul's Taxidermy". Now, I thought this was a side line you were into in the evenings, from all the animals you've run over at great speed, however your story of the rabbit suggests that the taxidermists are a completely different Annie and Paul, who probably aren't even riding a tandem.

Andy

28TH MAY, 2014

STAGE 14

Eskdalemuir to Penicuik

The forbidden road...

We had a great night's sleep and rest at the best of B&Bs courtesy of Jock and Roz. We can recommend it to anyone traveling through Scotland and, as I said, it turns out they will do evening meals for cyclists, so if ever you want to borrow the tandem for a quick jaunt then Watcarrick, just outside Eskdalemuir, is the place to stay.

I got in the habit of praying for our hosts whenever we left so I ventured into their kitchen and asked if they would allow me to pray for them and they seemed genuinely touched. Jock was very generous and gave us a packed lunch that would keep a small army on its feet for days.

And then we were off!

Quite slow as it happened due to the huge climbs and the significant head and side winds.

The first place of note we passed was the Kagyu Samye Ling Tibetan Buddhist Centre; the first to be established in the West, in 1967. Of course I had to take a photo or ten, and then we were off again.

We had arranged to meet a lady called May, a member of the local church that had paid for our stay in Watcarrick, in order to say thank you and let her know something of our adventure so far. Her farm was set off half a mile or so back from the road, and the lane leading to it would wreck our wheels if we attempted it on the tandem, and probably our ankles if we tried to walk in cleats[3]. Instead we stood and waved gaily, and, bless her, she got in her car and came to us.

If Mohammed won't go to the mountain...

I began to fall in love with Scotland from the moment we rode over the border; it is so open. I had imagined that the mountains would bear down on either side of us in a most intimidating manner but it isn't like that at all. There is so much space, truly beautiful.

I felt free.

---

[3] metal plates that attach the cycling shoes to the pedals

We passed within ten miles or so of Locherbie, a place that I would never have heard of had it not been for the awful tragedy there on December 21st, 1988. Two hundred and seventy people from twenty different nations lost their lives when a Pan Am airplane crashed there after a bomb detonated on board. To date I think it remains the worst terrorist attack and aviation disaster to have happened on British soil. It seemed not just crazy but impossible to understand that with all this landscape and wilderness around, the plane had to fall directly on the village. A mile or two either side and the appalling actions of that night would still have occurred with terrible loss of life but at least the village would have been spared.

The scenery in Scotland is breathtaking – have I mentioned that? – and even though the skies kept threatening to rain, it stayed away. It was still windy and damp, but this just added to the wildness and rugged beauty that is Scotland.

You would be forgiven at this moment if you thought the Scottish Tourist Board are paying me.

They aren't

Scotland really is something else.

We passed huge swathes of forest cut down for logging and I kept meaning to get off the bike and take a snapshot just to remember how striking the sight was. Mile after mile it went on with the added excitement of lorries occasionally bearing down on us, and then suddenly it was over and I had missed my opportunity.

We could have cycled back but in words similar to those of Margaret Thatcher,

"This girl's not for turning."

There were various signs along the road that we found intriguing, such as "deer crossing" – where? where?... never saw one! – and my personal favourite of "red squirrels crossing".

I could just imagine a little line of them heading over the road:

"Come on, Ginger, keep up; got to find those nuts you buried."

"Aw, Mum, do we have to?"

We were well on our way when we came across a sign that wasn't such a joy to encounter:

"ROAD AHEAD CLOSED. TAKE DIVERSION."

These signs are the stuff of cyclists' nightmares and, yes, a quick look at the GPS map told Paul that the diversion would add more than twenty miles to our journey.

This is OK in a car.

This is not OK on a bike when you have got to do sixty that day before detours, and to be fair even Paul balked at the idea – either that or telling me – and so he decided we would continue on the road we were travelling and see what happened.

I want to make it clear that this was *his* decision so that if we got in trouble I could use the 'Adam' excuse:

"But he said, and I did follow."

Everything seemed good at first and we thought we had got away with it until we came round a bend and ahead we saw a van, 'no go through' tape and signs, and three men standing like sentries.

Gingerly we approached.

The head honcho stepped forward like Gandalf in front of the Balrog: *YOOOO SHALLLL NOT PAAASSS.*

"If I let you through, I'll have to let everyone through," he moaned.

Come on! We were in a wilderness! Apart from the logging trucks twenty miles back and heading in the opposite direction, we hadn't seen a living soul all morning. He was hardly going to be inundated with cars, or even bikes, desperate to break through the cordon.

Whilst Paul engaged in a Camp David style summit meeting with this chap I rested the bike against a tree and tried to walk my sexiest best towards the other two workmen.

Failed miserably.

It is impossible to look sexy in undersized cycling gear and sweat pouring down your face. Worse still, when I took my helmet off there was no tossing my hair wildly like they do in commercials; it was plastered to my forehead.

I thought I would dump the sexy siren look and go for the helpless female instead.

"Oh, don't worry about him," they said. "He's just being a pain. We'll let you through."

Yay! It worked!

Paul in the meantime was wrapping up the talks with the guy whose opinion really mattered and after we promised faithfully to behave ourselves, and not sue if we got hit by a crane or stuck in tar for the rest of our lives, he reluctantly let us pass.

When we got to the actual work being carried out a mile or so up the road on a tiny bit of verge to the right of us that you could get a jumbo jet past, the workmen said a cheery hello and waved us through.

We had our first butty stop shortly after and held them suspended just before our lips as we saw another cyclist coming whizzing down the same route.

Whoops! Gandalf might have a busy day after all.

Several climbs later we got to Peebles and needed our coffee and cake fix, and then it was the last leg / wheel of the day to Penicuik. Unfortunately, it chose to rain, and rain heavily, from this point on.

As I kept telling Paul, the sun shines on the righteous so I can only assume that his thoughts were very naughty at this point, maybe on the lines of,

"I wish she was two stone lighter," or,

"Is she pedalling at the back?"

Dark thoughts indeed.

Peebles to Penicuik was hard work most of the way and the rain was not a welcome travelling companion. I insisted we stop and put our red tail light on, which Paul thought was completely unnecessary but I felt exceedingly vulnerable in the back seat. I also needed a wee-behind-a-tree stop, and my back was hurting furiously.

Years ago I damaged my back in a car collision, and have taken to having NST (Neural Structural Technique) treatment to ease the pain. This realigns the skeleton and muscles and works wonders, but I need it on a regular basis and seeing as I couldn't pack Natalie my therapist in our panniers, I was now suffering.

We arrived wet and weary after fifty-one miles and five hours in the saddle at our night stop in Penicuik to see our host Bruce waving to us at the window; though he could have been waving us away, it was difficult to tell through the rain.

We refused to leave and parked our tandem in the garage.

What a brilliant couple Bruce and Sally are! They were both officers in the army and were now in civvy street as teachers; Physics of all things!

I understand Physics less than French.

Go figure.

They were planning to leave teaching and go into full time foster caring and I could see them doing it; they are a down-to-earth, straightforward, hilarious, engaging couple.

As I bathed that night I found several beasties in my hair that had probably died from sheer boredom at the lack of pace that day, but, oh, it was good to relax in hot water and have the pick of Sally's toiletries.

Sally cooked us our first Scottish meal: venison with chestnuts, served with a handsome red wine and,

"Will yer tak a wee dram wi' yer for when yer away ta yer bed?"

I don't quite know why I've written that in a Scottish lilt; both Sally and Bruce are English.

When in Scotland do what the Scottish do – and so I had my first wee dram of whisky... and then my second.

After sleeping fourteen nights in fourteen different beds with various bedroom and bathroom configurations I was a little concerned that in the middle of the night after a toilet stop I would enter the wrong bedroom and climb in next to our hosts. I jokingly shared this with Sally who saw it as no laughing matter; she promptly led me to the landing and opened all the doors except their bedroom door so that I wouldn't get confused and wander in during the night.

We had climbed four Scottish hill ranges over one thousand feet on this day, and *I felt epic*.

Comments / Texts

Have a great day cycling thru Scotland.
Keep safe and hope weather is clear and dry for u to see
Scotland in all her glory. Had my best mountain walking
day ever there.

Jamie

Hi Annie and Paul. Praying for you, you're doing a
wonderful job! In difficult times I always think of my
grandad. He never gave up on anything. We called him
Spiderman. He wasn't particularly agile, just couldn't
get out of the bath! xx

David and Pam

Arrived wet and bedraggled but safe! Blog tonight. Back
having spasms please pray. Paul's hip LOADS better!

Annie (to Super 7)

Glad you've safely arrived – sounds like u need to look
after each other well this evening.

Hilary

Butties instead of haggis? What sort of a welcome was that?! Still, was the B&B comfy? Hungry at night? I do hope you went for the full English breakfast this morning just to show em. I would've. Anyways up hope it's not raining like it's been doing here. Gosh it's been so wet that the council have started clamping ducks and they now say it's here for the next month. No news like bad news I suppose especially in the British media.
Well, I'll give you a call later on to see how you're getting on with the tea breaks. Blessings.

Ian

Yo Bro! Sorry to have missed your call, we've been in the wild and windy mountains and often out of signal. We are safely deposited at our next stopover, arrived about half an hour ago tired and wet but happy to be alive and still in a good mood with each other! Thanx for all ur support Ian.

Annie

Glad u safe. Rained here solidly for last 3 days... Often sending up prayers that u are getting better weather than us... but now u are in Scotland probably no hope!

Pam

I can't believe how well u have done. I'm full of amazement & admiration! It's lovely to read your blog each day – still got your lovely sense of humour, an essential part of getting through any difficult situation. Humour helped Geoff & I thru his last year of cancer. It wud have been our 32nd anniversary tomorrow.
So Annie & Paul, make every second count.
I love seeing the little love signals & acts that go between U 2 in church.

Anne

Hi Annie. Looks like you two are burning up the miles on your tandem. Really well done. Alan & I look forward to meeting you on Sat.

Shona (future host)

Hello Shona! Lovely to hear from you! We are looking forward to meeting you and Alan too. With just a few days to go by then we will be in real celebratory mood... unless it rains!

Annie

Now I know why the Lord included that phrase in the prayer He taught ... "forgive us our trespasses", it was especially for you two! See how He loves you! Keep right on till the end of the road. Keep safe.

Bill and Marilyn

I'm full of admiration for your LEJOG challenge, but just thought I'd let you know about a lady MUCH older than yourselves at a staggering 67 years old passing through Macclesfield today who recently ran 21000 miles around the world in 5 years. Amazing!!... You've got a bit of catching up to do!!
Well done on all that climbing today!

Simon

Ooooooooh you naughty people! I reckon the Local Preachers' Course needs updating, to cover things like people who do naughty things on the Scottish mountain roads! We had some excitement today – we went to Biddulph Sainsbury's for once and our car played silly games and is going to the workshop on Wednesday for a new gear box – ouch!! That's what comes when you go forth (or fifth) and cross the border into the great unknown!

Catherine

Sounds like you had to work exceptionally hard today and you put those lovely red jackets to the test, although Paul looks like he is in training for the Grand National with the red jacket over his red spotty shirt – he just needs a crop now (Ian says to keep you pedalling at the back!)
The sun will have his Tam o' Shanter on for you over the next few Scottish days! Love and prayers.

Jude

You are such a laugh you two. Now we all heard via TV last night that a good old cycle ride will put ten whole years on your life! You should live to be a hundred by that reckoning.

Mum

29ᵀᴴ MAY, 2014

STAGE 15

Penicuik to Perth

You take the high road, can I take the train?

Due to Bruce and Sally being army folk, Paul and I wondered if it would be, "Stand by your beds!" at six in the morning, and toyed with the idea of sleeping in our cycling gear just in case, but they were very gentle with us and let us sleep in.

They had to leave before us to get to work so breakfast was a busy affair with everyone bustling around the kitchen but they left us the contents of their fridge to sort through for butty purposes and we were grateful for their kindness and lack of fuss. Bruce had put our other set of cycling clothes in for washing the previous day and they were hung up and dry.

174

Our shoes never got wet; we have overshoes, a sort of flexi-rubber boot thing that covers the entire shoe yet still allows us to clip our shoe cleats in and out of the pedals, and of course we had our bright red, ultralight weatherproof jackets that justified their cost of £95 each, again and again.

As we were the last to leave we were put in charge of locking up. The amount of times we checked our panniers to make sure "one last time" that we had packed everything had to be seen to be believed. Even so, there is still that terrible moment when you shut the door, post the key and think,

"Did I remember to pick up…"

To exit the garage Paul had to press a button at one end and then run and dive under the door as it slowly came down and I was there, camera in hand, to capture his personal Indiana Jones moment.

Penicuik is just south of Edinburgh and so we headed north into the big city and, believe me, it's big – the biggest we had cycled through so far. In fact, it took the whole morning just to cross Edinburgh. We didn't get lost and it wasn't particularly hairy to navigate through traffic; it's just that it's hilly and huge.

I'm not sure how much of the city Paul saw with his shoulders down and his head forward but I had a jolly good look-see from my perch at the back. We probably passed many important landmarks but I didn't know what I was looking at so the significance was lost on me, but I did pick out two. Edinburgh Castle was in the distance – too distant to even think about a photo – and Arthur's Seat rose high above the city surveying all beneath its feet.

In traffic we got stuck behind Mr White-van-man (he gets everywhere) and I had to chuckle when I read the logo; it was a company from St Awful in Cornwall.

Sorry, that's a typo, it should read St Austell.

Before you report me to the Cornish Mafia I have it on good authority from a Cornishman who lives there that its nickname is indeed St Awful, so I feel no shame.

It brought back all those difficult memories of the first few days of the tour. I was staggered to think how far we had come.

Gosh, in those early days I had kept crying and had moaned at all the hills...

I knew we were heading into the highlands of Scotland and started to mull over just how high would they be. I had steadfastly refused before then to even go there in my mind. I have a vivid imagination and the thought of Cornwall all over again but maybe worse brought me out in a cold sweat and we had to stop for coffee.

We sat on the kerb near a petrol station, cup in hand, and noticed that instead of white or yellow lines at the side of the road, this one was red.

Never seen that before. No idea what it meant. (Still no idea!)

Blood will be spilt if you stop here?

Blood *has* been spilt?

We were savvy enough to realize it probably meant something along the lines of, "Shoo-NOW!" so we beat a hasty retreat and merged back in with the traffic heading north.

The only problem we encountered that morning was regarding the Forth Road Bridge. We could see the darn thing but getting on it proved to be Mission Impossible. On the road leading towards it there was a diversion siphoning cyclists off to one side; the trouble was, it didn't siphon us back on again. We went round and round a roundabout so much so I thought of renaming myself Florence, and in desperation I dismounted, stood in the middle of the road and flagged down a car with "POLICE" written on it.

Good idea?

Nope.

It went straight past; didn't even see me. How could he *not* see a bright yellow banana woman gesticulating wildly in the road? Maybe they're used to that kind of behaviour in Edinburgh, I don't know, but I was near spitting feathers when a young woman in a little blue car came to our rescue.

She explained that someone had thoughtfully removed the diversion signs and we needed to head in such and such a direction through the Dalmeny Estate gardens and we would indeed find our way to the bridge and beyond.

This we did and actually it was a pleasant change to cycle through the beautiful grounds rather than be on roads, and of course I took the obligatory photo of the Mansion. It is a splendid Tudor Gothic Revival style mansion and home of the Earl of Rosebery.

I've been on Google, you can tell.

It's also one of the greatest treasure houses of Scotland, apparently, but we had no time to stop and stare; we were on a mission.

Everything was fine until the lane we were travelling down split in two and the signs made no sense. Whoever had thoughtfully removed the other diversion signs had obviously turned their keen attention to this place also.

Bless them. Really *bless them*.

We turned right, we pedalled, we became unsure, we asked a trucker – what was he doing there? – and he said we were on the right path. We then decided we were *not* on the right path and turned back. We asked a couple out walking who said the right fork was the scenic route. Such was our collective frame of mind by then that we didn't want scenic, we wanted *quick*, so we took left. Even then it wasn't straightforward and we had to chase down a fleeing postman for more directions before we eventually found ourselves on the bridge.

An easier way to describe our route through the estate would be to hand a crayon and a piece of paper to a two-year-old and then follow the resulting squiggle.

Crossing the Forth Road Bridge was a most awesome experience. The cycle track on the right went against the flow of traffic, or maybe there was one on the left side too but as sure as eggs are eggs we were not going to get off the bridge to try and get back on it again somewhere else. If we did it might suddenly disappear in Scotch mist and we would never get to John O' Groats.

The Forth Road Bridge is a suspension bridge spanning the Firth of Forth connecting Edinburgh at South Queensferry to Fife at North Queensferry. We witnessed the peculiar sight of workmen's disembodied heads suddenly popping up here and there in the track before us. Where was the rest of their body? They would disappear just as quickly. I should have taken a photo.

A huge volume of traffic thundered past us and we could literally feel the bridge bouncing beneath our wheels. By the time we got to the middle we seemed miles high from the water below and had crosswinds to tackle as well so we were bouncing all over the place; up and down *and* side to side, all whilst trying to avoid these appearing heads.

Through all this our eyes could not help but wander over continually to the impressive Forth Bridge carrying rail, which was adjacent to our position. I couldn't help but think it looked a far more solid structure than the one we were on and the trains weren't bouncing.

Despite the sea-sickness it was an incredible experience – one that I never dreamt I would ever do, so it wasn't exactly on my bucket list, but I crossed it off as a special achievement nonetheless.

By now it was past noon and we had been cycling for three hours so we stopped for lunch at the end of the cycle track by some bushes and used them to our advantage to cover our modesty whilst weeing.

We needed to get a wriggle on and after cycling through Inverkeithing it all seemed uphill for the next thirty miles, with the added dimension of 'significant localised wind'... I'll say no more but it did hamper our progress.

We stopped at Kinross for coffee, just in time for Ian to phone. Once again he suggested I write a book called The Grand Tea-Shop Tour of Britain. He's such a wag.

Derek phoned shortly after and said all the wonderful things about triumphing over adversity that I needed to hear, and that Ian should have said but didn't do for laughing.

I took to our daily coffee stops like a duck to water. Paul knows how to treat a girl:

"Come on a fifty-mile bike ride with me and I'll treat you to a cappuccino... with sprinkles!"

Be still, my beating heart.

I did get a little scratchy after a while with all these hills that Paul had planned en route, so much so that Paul actually stopped pedalling (he *never* stops pedalling), got off the bike (he *never* gets off unless he absolutely has to), took me in his arms and prayed loud and long over me.

Or maybe he was just checking that God realised what he was having to put up with.

Our destination in Perth was up a hundred hills and I did get scratchy some more – sorry Paul, sorry God. I texted our hosts for the night, Barry and Chris, to let them know we were coming, and – bless them! – they didn't do a runner but greeted us warmly when we arrived.

We'd only ever spoken on the phone prior to the tour but Chris and Barry had followed our blog and had taken to writing or texting the odd comment in the previous few days. I think they were possibly almost as excited as we were with our adventure, and it was like greeting old friends when we arrived on their doorstop.

All scratchiness vanished (I reserve that treat for Paul); we only had the stairs to climb that night, though I did share the bath with a spider and we both needed rescuing.

Whilst Chris and I chatted, the men gave the bike a thorough once over, and in the end we didn't head up for bed till nearly 9pm, which was late for us. Chris had read the blog I posted about possible midnight wanderings and had given us an en suite so that they could sleep easy in their bed that night.

Comments / Texts

Morning peddlers,
The riding crop thing is nothing to do with me as I would never suggest that you Annie are not pulling your weight. Remember the old adage; "behind every good man is a good woman pushing him forward". No it's not the woman with the whip (which is every man's fantasy – is it still raining by the way?) that worries me, it's the frying pan that usually announces you've done something wrong. Well I do hope that your stay was a good one and that you are up and ready this morning. I must say that we are intrigued by your hosts over the border; first a Jock and then a Bruce, I wouldn't be surprised if you don't have a Willie tonight. Anyways up, have a great day cycling. God speed and bless you both.

Ian

I remember standing with you over 25 yrs ago looking at the forth rd bridge. Paul and I have just cycled over it! Amazing. xx

Annie (to Malcolm)

Am relaxing in bath after long hard slog today, now in Perth.

Annie (to Super 7)

My Margaret doesn't like 'sprinkles' on her coffee. You know what they say about Scots and Yorkshire folk being a bit tight with their 'brass'! It looks as if the folk over the border are looking after you very well – venison indeed!

I can share my 1964 experience of the Forth Road Bridge with our Morris 1000 and me driving on 'L' plates. I was touring Scotland with my parents and using this holiday for driving practice. We saw a few cars on the bridge and I drove up to the pay booth only to find the bridge was still being built! The cars on the bridge were belonging to the workmen doing the construction. We had to find another route – no sat navs in those days, just a book of maps. You may well have gone faster than the good old Morris – we did manage 50mph up the A1 on our way to Scotland but we did have our luggage too on board.

John and Margaret

We are trying as hard as we can to get to you! Headwinds and hills are slowing us down! We're in Kinross having a coffee fix. We will b with you asap.

Annie (to Chris and Barry)

We have been thinking of you & know it will be very tough going thru Fife & that bit of Perthshire. C u when u arrive. xx

Chris and Barry

Perth, that is amazing! Ian said he had spoken with you today; it must have been really something crossing the Firth of Forth bridge even with the crosswinds buffeting against you! How is your back? We prayed for your healing last night and gave thanks for Paul's improved hip. You are beginning the final purple spectrum on your map – not far to bring in the PINK! Have another blessed evening. Lots of love to your Perth 'family'.

Jude

Back is a lot better, Paul's hip no problem...
the power of prayer even at a distance!
After talking with Ian every day for two weeks I feel
I have to say to you: Jude you're a brave woman!

Annie

"Where are the hills, it looks very flat in the blog
pictures, not a hill in sight" (says Ian)!
Glad to hear Paul is treating his woman right but
Ian thinks that the sprinkles are a little extravagant.
He says that now you are in Scotland, Paul should
be learning to rein in his wallet a bit more!
I am sure Ian must believe that we live in Scotland
then! Good journey for tomorrow and trusting
your back is better now Annie as we prayed for it
at the prayer group last night.
Prayer already answered with Paul's hip.
Love and blessings. xxxx
Oh, and I have just read your text
and I am VERY brave.

Jude (with comments from Ian)

B

Jude

...B?...

Annie

I don't know how that happened. I was busy writing on your blog so it is either a letter of significance or I caught my finger on the key pad and then managed to send it!

Jude

Wow! Perth. Who knew there was 5 days cycling north of Perth. But hey u only have days... so so close!

Pam

Kinross eh? My dad was stationed there in his national service days! I hasten to add we never did visit Scotland after his experience. "Bleak, miserable and cold" was a polite way of saying what he remembered about the place! I can't believe how far you've gone... you'll be able to see the light at the end of the chimney soon! (Well you are going up) I pray that all your aches and pains subside... perhaps you should start putting a wee dram in your cappuccino! Have a good night's rest.

Helen

Take care travelling to Scotland; it's a long way. I can say that with some authority! So looking forward to seeing you next Tuesday!

Annie (to Shirley)

That blog was a laugh out loud read! Love it!

Natalie

I saw a documentary once that showed it took a year to paint the Forth Bridge, kinda think you were quicker across it than a lick of paint! It is amazing how far up you are. Am still singing your song – every day. Lots of love to you both, bless you.

Mum

30TH MAY, 2014

STAGE 16

Perth to Calvine

"Face to face we meet at last, great pudding Chieftain, what a blast!"

These are not the words that our hosts for tonight met me with, though I was piling on the pounds (must be muscle).

Rather these words are to signify that this night would be the one we would meet a true Scottish haggis.

But more of that later...

I would have been happy to sit with Chris all day in their comfy chair drinking tea and talking with that easy knack women possess, but Paul was having none of it. Barry sacrificed his best lettuce in the garden for our butties which really was above and beyond the call of duty and we could give nothing in return except our heartfelt thanks. When I prayed for them, Barry was quite moved, a little teary even; it was so easy to warm to this gentle couple.

Rejuvenated by a good night's sleep we shot along like a bullet from a gun and all was good for at least, oh, four miles.

For months before the tour Paul spent many hours planning our route down to the last bush. He had even used Google to look at the Street View image of many of the roads and lanes so he knew just what to expect, and had done a superb and necessary job. The route showed up on his GPS as a thin blue line which we followed diligently and, for most part, successfully.

So when we came to the end of a road with a choice of left sailing down and right heading up a steep hill my heart fluttered with delight when he said,

"Signal left!"

Life was good. An enjoyable day lay ahead of us. We were happy, we were in love, we were on an adventure, and in high spirits we merrily zoomed down the hill. Cycling doesn't get much better than this; the birds were singing, the sun was shining, it was a beautiful day.

Until we got to the bottom.

Paul's shoulders slumped, his head went down, and his pedalling slowed. I knew in my heart of hearts what he would say before he ever uttered the words:

188

"Whoops! We should have gone right."

D'oh!

The sun hid and the birds went silent; even they knew this was not a good moment in our marriage.

Once recovered from that little hiccup we ventured on to Dunkeld via the cycle track, and took in the majestic sight of Dunkeld Cathedral dominating the skyline of this pretty Perthshire village. It was here we also made our first introduction with the River Tay, the longest river in Scotland and one that we would meet again under its different guises. We stopped for our gold dust butties in the stunning surroundings of Dunkeld gardens. The weather really was most pleasant, and ready to continue, we followed the cycle route and got hopelessly lost.

Just when I thought we were forever doomed to go round and round the rhododendrons, a kindly soul took pity on us and pointed to the exit.

From there we made our way up to Pitlochry which proved quite a climb but the scenery made up for the struggle. The Scottish do look after their cyclists and the cycle tracks are great to travel along, and better than in England, dare I say.

Pitlochry is a busy town and I was nervous as we navigated our way through. Our bladders were screaming at us for a pit-stop, which made concentration all the harder, so we dismounted as delicately as we could by Victoria's Restaurant and took it in turn to walk ever so carefully to the toilets. I couldn't help but notice they did my favourite cake – millionaire slice – so we took the opportunity and sat in the sun with cake and coffee in hand.

The restaurant owner happened to be passing and, taking an interest in the tandem, she fell in to conversation with us. When she heard we were cycling LEJOG for charity and we gave her a flyer to show the route, she promptly waived the bill and in that moment I resolved to tell every future coffee shop our intent from here on in.

Unfortunately, we were never shown that particular kindness again.

Leaving Pitlochry proved an uphill slog; we saw snow-capped mountains in the distance which I thought very striking and dramatic until I realised we would probably be cycling up one of them the next day. They instantly lost some of their appeal.

To be fair, the Scottish seem to try as far as they can to build roads *between* the mountains rather than *up* them, and even though cycling through the highlands is an uphill journey, it's not as bad as it could be and you do develop climbing legs. You may climb four hundred feet but then it levels out a bit before the next climb, and its nothing like Cornwall which is just up-down-up-down the whole way.

Dragons teeth.

To all Cornish folk reading this, let me be honest: Cornwall by car or motorbike or train or helicopter or, let's face it, *anything with an engine* is breathtakingly beautiful.

On a pedal bike it's just breathtaking.

At least, that is my experience. Please go ahead and prove me wrong.

Scotland is a totally different scenario and one that personally I enjoyed a whole heap of mountains more.

Both Derek and Ian phoned within minutes of each other; they swear it was pure chance. Usually it was Ian that said the outrageous, the tongue-in-cheek, the teasing words, but this particular day Derek excelled himself, and the sad thing is, he was being serious.

"I bet that once you've reached John O' Groats you'll be that chuffed that you'll just want to cycle straight back down again!"

In which universe is he living?

Our resting place for the night was to be the Struan Inn, about twelve miles north of Pitlochry and on the edge of the Cairngorms National Park. On the way we passed near to the historic castle at Blair Atholl, home to the Atholl Highlanders, a Scottish ceremonial infantry regiment. The sign at the roadside showed one of these Atholl highlanders in full regalia. I shouted to Paul,

"See, real men cycle in kilts."

We reached the Struan Inn at 3pm having made good speed and were met by a sign hanging in the window:

"Sorry, we are closed."

Not as sorry as I was.

Possibly driven on by the chilling thought of a mad Annie on his hands, Paul kept his finger on the buzzer until they answered the door and let us in.

Our en suite was just heaven and after a shower I lay on the bed for a good long while. I got quite tearful thinking how far we had come: from the seed of an idea, the planning, the organizing places to stay, the leafleting, the charities, and then to be experiencing this unbelievable journey with Paul, of hills and valleys, and towns and cities, good times and bad, the people, the laughter, the new friends, all the encouragement we had received in blogs and texts and phone calls – yes, even Ian's.

I also got quite tearful when I realized just how much my bottom hurt. To begin with we had used our special bottom cream sparingly, applying it just once in the morning and again in the afternoon. I was now at the stage of applying it liberally morning, noon and night-time, after showers, before bed and up to my armpits for added protection.

Shiny clean and squeaking I sat in the lounge like a lady of leisure and read a coffee-table book about Loch Ness, while Paul did the usual bike checks, before turning my attention to the blog I wrote every night for our internet followers.

We took a stroll down to the river and bridge. Very picturesque.

As much as I loved meeting new hosts every night, it was precious to spend this time with just Paul for company. I am the extravert of the two of us – did you guess that? – and meeting new people is always exciting for me, whereas Paul is way more reserved. My minister Derek had taken me to one side before the tour and gently pointed out that Paul may not be up to talking to new folk as much as I would be, which in usual circumstances would be true, but he had done himself proud and had thrown himself into the social scene in a way that quite surprised me.

But for now is was just the two of us and it was enchanting to be standing with him in happy content listening to the water bubble over the rocks, lost in our own world.

We sauntered back for dinner. I have only had haggis once in my life and not well cooked haggis at that. Paul, on the other hand, had never tasted it and as it was on the menu I really thought we should give it a go. Mary-Ann, the owner, took our order.

"What's it like?" enquired Paul.

Without stopping to engage brain I said,

"Oh, it's just like stuffing, really."

How I wasn't thrown out on the spot is a miracle.

We had cycled forty-three miles on this day with only 4.10hrs spent in the saddle. Our total mileage now stood at 801. Better than that, we only had *4 days to go!*

Comments / Texts

Well done. Up and at 'em for another day on the road.
Keep those wheels rolling!
Prayin for u and yr safety particularly. x

Jamie

Hi both, hope you had a good sleep last night as I fear you will need it today. The dreaded Grampians! (Is it the Grampians up there or am I getting them confused with Snowden?) Still, it's going to be steep, whichever it is, so I am praying for you like a man possessed. Can I say that I wonder?
I am in the Derbyshire dales this morning enjoying the picturesque views of the White Peak and it's beautiful in a soft undulating sort of way, but you're heading for mountainous rocky crags and shear escarpments with the occasional raptor gliding on invisible thermals. Just remember that its beauty is in its drama and I'm sure you'll love it. However, it might be best to get everyone you can to pray, like I'm doing. God's love and courage to you both and don't let the devil win as he's a wuss. Blessings. Think of the money you're raising!

Ian

Thank u for those encouraging words...!

Annie

Glad I could be of assistance.

Ian

Arrived safe in Calvine tired but happy, a good day's cycling. 4 days to go!

Annie (to Super 7)

I am so pleased and relieved as it looked like a really mountainous ride from the map.
You are actually deep purple now and heading into the almost pink tomorrow!
Well done guys and keep praising God for totally being with you even through the toughest times.

Jude

Daniel just stated that it was REALLY funny that you are STILL on your bike ride! Riding his own bike, he went headfirst into a bush as he couldn't decide which way to go. Hopefully your GPS will save you such shame!

Pam

Just read your blog...
maybe GPS wouldn't help Daniel after all!

Pam

I am so thrilled for you both, what an amazing day... glad your marriage is growing stronger by the turn of your pedals... keep on... 4 more days... I don't believe it!

Rhona

Only 4 days left – that is amazing – where has the time gone?? You'll be cycling on air now – knowing that you are so close to the goal – well done both of you! Hope you've ordered champagne at John O' Groats?

Geoff and Janette

Haha, Annie, I can just imagine your reaction to having to go back up the hill! Praying for you. xx

Jonny

The haggis! Och aye! Has to enter with the playing of bagpipes, or a bowed head and eaten with due reverence – IT IS NOT STUFFING!!

Mum

31ST MAY, 2014

STAGE 17

Calvine to Carrbridge

I am officially in love with Scotland!

Neither of us slept well that night at the Struan Inn (nothing to do with the haggis, which was delightful in the extreme), I woke up several times in fear and trembling thinking about the huge climb we faced up Drummochter Pass, and woke Paul to share the love. Situations always seem worse in the middle of the night, don't they? Even with my imagination held in check though, I was sure the pass would be equivalent to the north face of the Eiger, and played 'loo, loo, skip to the loo' all night.

The breakfast menu looked scrumptious and in another lifetime I would have worked my way through it with inspiring determination; however, we just ate toast.

The breakfast room was impressive with weapons and shields and all things Scottish hung on the walls. I asked Mary-Ann to pose for me with the usual sign – "We put Paul and Annie up" – but unfortunately I didn't get the camera angle right and it looked as though she was walking about the place with a ceremonial sword stuck in her head.

We had to pay for our butties. I said in my bestest and brightest voice,

"We're doing this for charity!"

It didn't work. We still had to pay.

We should have packed a doggy bag with half the breakfast menu contained therein.

My back was desperately painful so Paul massaged it, and prayed for me, for himself, for "the ride today", for the bike, and for any possible eventuality that might come our way on this most auspicious of days.

I think I prayed, "Help!" or "Ouch!" or something like it.

I procrastinated on the toilet a good deal longer than usual and smothered myself in 'Forever' perfume, thinking that is how long the day would seem. All this faffing about meant that we didn't set off until nearly 10am.

We stood outside in glorious sunshine which was at odds with my sense of foreboding. After a false start with the pedals in the wrong position we set off and wobbled down the lane before I had to dive behind a bush.

My apprehension of the climb could not have been farther from the reality. The Drummochter Pass was sheer magnificence! We took it slowly – no change there, then – and spent the whole time pointing out the stunning views to each other, puncturing the air with, "Wow!" and, "Spectacular!" and, "Oh my goodness!" such was the landscape before us. The titanic mountains of the Cairngorms, some capped with snow, stood silently basking in our praise as we cycled through. I took numerous photos which did not do justice to what we were experiencing all around us so I gave up in the end and just soaked up the atmosphere instead.

This is the moment I fell in love with Scotland.

We followed the cycle track which runs alongside the A9 all the way to the top, where we stopped to take photos by the sign that reads, "Drummochter Summit. 1516 feet (462 meters) above sea level."

Here we met two other cyclists who were also doing LEJOG as part of a group organised by CTC[4]. The club gives everyone a gismo with the map on it for the route that day and each person cycles at their own pace while the tour bus takes their luggage to the next overnight stop. I had to fight off waves of jealousy

---

[4] Cyclists' Touring Club

when I heard that bit. They were duly impressed we were carrying our luggage with us.

So was I, though I still felt jealous.

We straight away fell into conversation about cycling up the length of Britain as if we had known each other all our lives, such is the camaraderie that LEJOG inspires.

I've experienced that before when I went to a 'trekkie' convention in London to watch the then five Star Trek films back to back.

I digress.

We discovered that this group of about twenty riders would be staying in the same hotel as us, when and if we ever got to John O' Groats. We met more of the group that day, though their route would eventually take them through Stirling and up across the top of Scotland via Thurso, whereas we were heading up the east coast.

Over the top of the pass we then had the first glorious descent towards Dalwhinnie. We couldn't go as fast as we would have liked as the cycle track still undulated and there were several wooden slatted bridges to cross over. We wobbled a bit as we headed down the track. It was the old A9, before they built the new one next to it, and was a little uneven in places, and we didn't want to take a tumble. The other reason may lie in the fact that the fumes from the Dalwhinnie Whisky distillery were circling our heads but once we moved on to the present day A9 we rocketed along, passing several of the other cyclists.

We may go slow up the hills but, by gum, we drop like a stone!

One of the group took a photo of us as we hurtled by at lightning speed. I saw him pointing the camera in our direction so I sat up and waved. When we bumped into him days later at the hotel in John O' Groats he recognised us and after swapping e-mail addresses posted the photo to us. You can see Paul working really hard in the front and me happily waving at the back. It's my favourite photo of the tour.

I'm not sure I was pedalling though.

We stopped for a well earned and thoroughly enjoyable butty stop at a wayside cafe near Dalwhinnie.

I've mentioned Dalwhinnie four times now; I like how it sounds and its composition of letters.

Maybe I'm still drunk on the whisky fumes.

Apart from having a luxury 'comfort stop' in a proper toilet, I took the opportunity to telephone friends of ours who were holidaying in Scotland. They suggested we meet up somewhere south of Inverness, and we decided on Feshiebridge.

Back on the tandem we set off and rode through the glorious country that is Scotland. On our way through Kingussie we passed a great ruin of a castle or monastery (or something) on the hill. We didn't have time to explore though; we were meeting friends and I was super excited.

Our chain came off twice in that short space of time. Blogs that friends had sent earlier in the tour related to a line from one of

Charles Wesley's songs – "My chains fell off, my heart was free." – and I could hear them singing it with gusto in my head now. But my heart was *not* free, my heart was downcast and I relayed this fact to Paul with amazing clarity.

Fortunately, "he knows bike secrets" too and got us moving again.

We saw our friend David before he saw us; he was standing in the shade by the roadside reading a book. Paul warned me not to jump off the bike in my enthusiasm:

"If you do, we'll topple over."

That didn't stop me and I did, but we didn't... just.

Feshiebridge was idyllic to cycle through, nestled in a beautiful forest against the backdrop of the magnificent Cairngorm Mountains. There are trails to gently walk along by the river, not that we did, and perfect picnic sites to enjoy. The Scottish Forestry Commission say that there are sculptures hiding amongst the trees; we didn't see them (obviously going way too fast). We did in fact have the perfect picnic there as we shared David and Rachel's butties with them and they broke out the Irn Bru, which I think is the equivalent of champagne in Scotland.

David cycles everywhere in Macclesfield and up into the surrounding hills on his 'Brook's' saddle; a firm leather saddle with no added cushioning or air holes, just a rock solid seat.

He has my undying respect.

We were on our final leg of the day through Aviemore and then just a few miles on to our resting place in Carrbridge, the home of Alan and Shona.

We stopped for yet another coffee at The Happy Haggis; not exactly five-star rating but we were happy along with the haggis so that was OK.

Paul telephoned Alan from here, who let us know how to find his house:

"It's set back from the road with a silver truck in the driveway."

He added that seeing as we were in Aviemore, we might like to pop in on the local Red Cross shop as Shona was the manageress there.

Paul said yes.

Seeing as the Red Cross is a charity shop dealing in second hand goods, I suggested we leave the bike there.

Paul said no.

Just to let you know, Aviemore train station has to be the prettiest station I have ever seen, at least from the outside. It would have been nice to see it on the inside whilst buying a ticket to the top of Scotland but that was never going to happen, was it? And to be fair, with just three days to go we knew we were on a winner, barring serious mishap. The weather had been kind too; to be honest, God knows what I am like when it's raining and out of deepest sympathy with Paul kept it away.

After fifty-six miles and five hours of actual pedalling we arrived in Carrbridge, where we soon discovered that every house is set back from the road with a silver truck in the driveway...

It's interesting what you learn about people in conversation over a meal. For example, Alan used to live in Dunblane and nearly went out with Andy Murray's mum, Judy, when she was fifteen.

I nearly went out with Donny Osmond when I was thirteen; only the small problem of distance kept us apart.

We ate salmon with potatoes, beans and salad, followed by rhubarb pie, ice-cream, cheese and biscuits. It's no wonder I put on weight; the real mystery is how I managed to fit in to my ever shrinking cycling shorts. If Lionel Bart hadn't already penned the song 'Food, Glorious Food', I'm sure I would have got round to it at some point.

We spent an enjoyable evening that night with Shona and Alan and a very laid-back terrier called Buster. They were so encouraging of what we were doing, and were no strangers to adventure themselves; Alan had sailed his trimaran round Britain the previous summer! This made me ponder the meaning of life and I decided that cycling was a much better bet. Paul's heart soared, thinking I had finally fallen in love with life on two wheels, until I pointed out that really it was a choice between a rock and a hard place.

Snuggled in bed that night I did admit to Paul that this had been the best day cycling ever, and that we had to come back to Scotland in the future.

"But not on a bike," I added quickly.

Comments / Texts

Good morning you two!
It's the blinking Cairngorms not the Grampians as they are in Victoria, Australia! Better weather by the looks of it but a long way off your track.
The Cairngorms are still as breathtaking and awe inspiring though which is something to remember as you're pedalling up them. I was hoping to see some beautiful pictures of the scenery on your blog, as Annie said she's a wizard at taking photos while talking on the phone and cycling.
What's happened? Call yourself a woman? Come on, multi-tasking should be second nature.
Tonight I expect great vistas including the panoramic function. Anyways up I have a song for you to sing while you're on your way today; it's 'The Only Way Is Up' by Yazz and the Plastic Population. I think you'll love it. Blessings to you both, extended family in our Lord Jesus Christ. Speak to you later.

Ian

We are definitely going to have a coffee and cake, and if necessary a wine, to get us through the Cairngorms.

Annie

All sounds great, but how will a cake help you cycle up a hill?

Ian

Energy, man, energy!

Annie

Arrived safe, now in bath. 56 miles thru the Cairngorms.
Best day ever! Amazing scenery, tired now though!

Annie (to Super 7)

We hope you had tatties and neeps with your haggis
last night, and remember, IRN BRU is made from
GIRDERS! So you will be powered up for the last 3 days!
It is also bright orange so that will also help with your
energy levels!

Jude

With haggis AND Irn Bru, you two may never walk the
same way again!!

Catherine

1ˢᵀ JUNE, 2014

STAGE 18

Carrbridge to Allness

Keeping up with the Joneses.

For some reason I didn't sleep well this night either and woke with a sore belly and a sore head. Shona, Alan and Buster walked with us to the historic packhorse bridge just up the road from their house and from which the village gets its name. It was built in the 1700s but wear and tear and misuse have since made it unstable. Apparently locals and tourists alike used to jump off it into the River Dulnain below.

I wasn't keen.

In olden days coffins used to be taken over it on the way to the church but now no one was allowed to walk on it, and even though it had stood the test of time, it did look in danger of imminent collapse. Very picturesque though, so Alan took a photo of us with our backs to it before we said our goodbyes. Then he videoed us lurching unsteadily away on the bike up the road.

There is always a moment on the tandem when we push off, and before we have synchronised our pedalling and balance, when we are never quite sure if we are going to sally forth or go belly up.

On this day we were headed up the Slochd pass. I couldn't believe anything could better the Drummochter experience of the day before.

And I was right.

It was still beautiful, don't get me wrong, but Drummochter had captured my heart.

On the way up we saw our first wild deer. Everywhere there are signs cautioning road users about deer but we had never seen one of these elusive animals up to this point.

It would have been a far happier encounter had it been alive but, alas, it was dead. Even so I approached it and spent time marvelling at its colouration and chiselled perfection; even in death these animals look very serene and delicate to me.

We slogged up the Slochd pass and took a breather at the top (as well as several on the way up, if I'm honest). The A9 is at a height of 1,328 feet here and it's the second highest place on the route from Perth to Inverness, the highest being my beloved Drummochter at 1,500 feet (460 metres). The Highland main railway line uses the pass and we saw several trains snaking their way through the wilderness.

All that climbing put us in need of food and drink so we leant our bike against a corner wall in Castletown and opened our top box, just as another tandem flew past.

When they saw us they backpedalled, so to speak (impossible in real life), dismounted and had lunch with us. Carlene and Bill were American and doing the tour with the CTC bunch.

We talked all things tandem. "How long have you had yours?" "Do you pedal on the back?" "What is your seat like?" "Is Carlene ever allowed on the front? No, me neither."

They had transported their tandem by plane to England, which we found quite astonishing. I didn't feel that I would want to put my trust in a bike that came in three pieces, but they were happy enough.

Meeting them would later prove to be a godsend when we got to John O' Groats...

Apart from meeting Bill and Carlene, the day had been pretty uneventful but we still had Inverness to negotiate and that would prove to be no mean feat. In times when not much is happening other than pedalling I amuse myself by working out how many different positions I can hold the handle bars in.

I made it thirteen.

I challenge you.

On the way to Inverness we could have got drunk on the fumes of the whisky distilleries in the area there too.

"Drunk in charge of a tandem" sounds like a Chance card in Monopoly with "Go directly to jail" added.

We were fortunate, there were no police about; in fact the only people we spoke to or even saw that morning were the CTC crew who all bombed passed us travelling to Inverness as well.

I swear town planners plan diversions that go absolutely nowhere just for the fun of it.

"Let's make them go round and round… and round again."

I'm sure I saw a Nigel Planer skit on it once and it has never been truer than in the city of Inverness. There were detours, diversions and road closures all over the shop, and somehow we ended up in the toilets at M&S; that's how confusing the signs were.

We finally broke away from all the madness and made it over the Kessock bridge to freedom and sanity.

Paul had planned the next part of our route using the A9 which was heavy with traffic, and I was less than pleased. We stopped at Tore for him to work out another route off the beaten track but it would be longer, and I was less than pleased again.

Being in direct contact with God, who is in direct contact with Derek the trucker, was useful to Paul at this moment because my phone rang just as I was gearing up for my best 'Chernobyl Annie' impression:

"Why did you bring us out onto the A9 to die? We should have stayed in Inverness."

Derek spent twenty minutes perfecting his 'personal trainer' chat on me. He was able to say things to me that it wouldn't have been wise for Paul to say given our close proximity. Derek probably had a stiff drink after that conversation, but he did coax me back on the bike, and when Paul navigated our way to Dingwall we had coffee and cake and the world took on a brighter hue, at least in that moment.

On we continued and after a while, when the need for a wee transcended all other thoughts, we had to stop again. I was desperate but there were no trees to hide behind and no comfy grass verge to nestle in. With the occasional car driving past I had to suspend my very vulnerable behind over a bank of thistles.

Prayers to my Maker were desperate:

"Please, oh please, don't let me lose balance."

Everything between my neck and my ankles hurt, so when we finally arrived in Allness after fifty-three miles, and five hours spent in the saddle, plus numerous stops and anger management issues, I was fragile to say the least. Realizing this, Paul thought it best if he walked up the driveway and met the family first, to give me time to compose myself. The other reason being that we weren't entirely sure this was actually the right house and the last thing either of us wanted was for me in my condition to walk up the long steep drive just to discover we had to walk back down it again.

The whole family came to the door and waved cheerily to me and I tried desperately to send an equally jolly wave back, but I was close to tears and it must have looked as though I had a broken arm as only a small part of my wrist had any capability of movement. It would have been a lot easier if they had then all trooped back inside but instead they all stood smiling and expectant, and I knew I couldn't wave at them for the next three hours; I had to move.

I tried desperately not to walk like John Wayne up the garden path – and failed miserably. Nine hundred miles in the saddle does that to a girl.

Rob Jones is the minister of the Church of Scotland in Allness and he and his wonderful wife Jo welcomed us warmly (and gently, in my case) into their home. While Paul showered, I sat on the kitchen stool and drank about three pints of tea which started my recovery process; they plied me with cake too which helped.

This is where I met the next Scottish love of my life: tablet. It's a fudge type tray bake that melts in the mouth and – oh, my goodness! – it is delicious.

Conversation didn't stop for a minute. Their son Mark and his wife Sarah were visiting along with their little son Matthew, and everything was going on at about a hundred miles an hour which, funnily enough, was just what I needed.

Jo took me to the guest bedroom which had a lopsided male toilet sign on the door. I entered with some trepidation. *Phew!* No urinals, just a lovely comfy bed.

Bathed and changed, I came downstairs a new woman – almost. We were both very tired so when Rob asked if we'd like to go with him to church that night, we replied that our spirits were willing but our bodies were shot.

After a delicious tea of broccoli, chicken pie and self-assembly Pavlova for dessert, we spent an hour or so before bed laughing with Mark and Sarah, who fed me more cake. God bless them.

It had been a difficult day and when we hit the sack at only just gone 8pm, I asked Paul if we could do something easier next year like swim with sharks.

Comments / Texts

Dear Annie and Paul, today we celebrate the Ascension of the Lord. 'May God enlighten the eyes of your mind so that you can see what hope his call holds for you, what rich glories he has promised the saints will inherit, and how infinitely great is the power he has exercised for us believers.' (Ephesians 1: 17-23) Sending you both much love.

Maz

Hi! Safe. Shattered, hard day today, bit fragile.
Now both clean and resting.
Thanx 4 prayers, they were well needed.

Annie (to Super 7)

You are my heroes! It will be worth it in the end.
You have been brilliant!

Pat

So glad that you are safely settled for the evening with your wonderful chain of hosts. Much prayer for you both today as always – The Lord is always on your side no matter how tough and steep the road is.
TWO MORE DAYS TO GO! Your sister will be packing the car up ready for her momentous journey north – you will be together very SOON.
Lots of love to you, Paul, and your hosts. xxx

Jude

Is Sunday night youth group on tonight?

Joe (teenager)

I don't know Joe... I'm in Scotland!
Best ask another leader!

Annie

O, Ok.

Joe

Nearly there! You have done so well. Get the tissues ready Paul for when you reach the end! (Annie may need them too.) You have both done amazingly!

Charlotte

Annie, you may be tired and really pi**ed off with the slog, but you write a great blog and keep me personally in hoots of laughter, bless you. Two days to go and the cavalry are winging their way.

Mum

It is purely because you sound so cheery in your blogs that everyone (including Paul) thinks you'll be ready to do it all the way down again... although Paul has seen the reality moment by moment, so he should possibly know better! 2 days... 2 days... WOW!!! xxxxx

Pam

Don't forget to stop at John O' Groats – don't think your navigation system is waterproof to take you on to the Orkney and Shetland Islands!! Is the tandem amphibious? (Needed the dictionary for that word!) You are now farther north in Scotland than I (John) have ever ventured. Seriously what a great team you are!

Sue has been busily rounding up the troops for your 'welcome home party' next Saturday – particularly in the cakes department – we just happened to be passing Makro yesterday, so we called in for a free coffee and thought of you and got some flapjacks!

Our minister Derek was reminding us about Ascension Day and Pentecost at Wellspring this morning and to illustrate this for us we went outside and the youngsters released a balloon which floated up into the sky. The balloon said "Jesus" on it and we joked it was heading to Biddulph although some thought it was aiming for John O' Groats! It was purple coloured if you spot it up there! As ever, we continue to uphold you in prayer and will await your return with great eagerness and joy. God bless.

John and Margaret

You are doing brilliantly and we are totally hooked on your entertaining blogs (any chance of keeping these up when you return home...) Nearly there, very excited for you and can't wait to hear about the next two days. Please keep eating cake, I have come to the conclusion that it is a crucial component when cycling.

Andy and Bev

2ND JUNE, 2014

STAGE 19

Allness to Helmsdale

"Let them eat cake!"

Paul rose in the middle of the night for a toilet stop. What *is* it with us and our bladders? He was very good; he didn't search for a bush, which is our usual trick, he used the bathroom across the hall instead.

When he returned he warned me,

"Be careful of the wooden slatted step by the bath. If you hit your toe on it, you might break a bone and won't be able to cycle."

I had to fight the urge to run to the bathroom there and then and kick it as hard as I could.

After a good night's sleep we emerged for an early breakfast with the family. Rob met me at the bottom of the stairs.

"Bad news, Annie, the tandem's still in the garage."

D'oh!

We haven't asked much from our hosts over the last three weeks, just the basics:

- Somewhere safe to store the bike overnight.
- A bath / shower and, "Can we use your toiletries, and have you any towels?"
- A meal, with copious cups of tea and coffee.
- "Do you mind if we ignore you for half an hour whilst we sort the blog and pictures?"
- "Please, don't be offended that we go to bed early, and can we have a cup of hot milk each? Oh, and could you put all our stuff in the washing machine? But don't use conditioner or the tumble drier."
- "If you wouldn't mind hanging it up for us, that'd be great. We'll be in bed by then."

- "Yes, please, breakfast at eight. Just cereal. No, really. Can we have butties and drink for the journey? No cheese for Paul, sorry."
- "Can you possibly recharge our batteries for all our different gismos?"
- And bananas, lots of bananas.

It has taken a special type of people to put us up / put up with us.

At breakfast the little lad Matthew cried whenever we laughed so the poor mite spent most of the time in tears, even though we all tried really hard to be serious. It would have been a joy to have gotten to know Rob and Jo better; they are the only couple that we were not able to spend any real time with, which was a huge shame because they were funny, genuine, caring people.

Paul suggested to me that the next time we did LEJOG we would make the time.

I'm sure you can hazard a guess at my response to that, and I mean that as no offense to Rob and Jo; it was the LEJOG bit that warranted a swift and clear reply.

Somehow the toilet system blocked up that morning and I had to use the church toilets next door. It meant Rob having to come with me, unlock and show me where to go. I said I was quite happy to duck behind a tree but he smiled sweetly and said that it really wouldn't be a problem.

I told him not to wait. If the last eighteen days were anything to go by, I could be there a while.

The family prayed with us, which was a privileged experience — for us not them, I mean — and then Jo left for work, but not before packing the contents of half a cake shop in our panniers.

And then we were off for our penultimate day in the saddle. As we left, Sarah said, "Don't worry about the A9. It's got nothing on the mums dropping kids off to school at the bottom of the road!" and she was right.

Our spirits were high as we cycled that morning. The farther we headed up the A9, the less traffic there was; what with that and the stunning scenery we were definitely enjoying the ride. We hadn't seen a single road sign with "John O' Groats" written on it and I was a little suspicious that maybe we were slightly lost.

And then suddenly — there it was!

"John O' Groats. 85 miles."

Clearly this was another photo call, so Paul held his hands high in celebration that he only had to drag me for another eighty-five miles.

With twenty miles' cycling under our belt we crossed over the Dornoch bridge and rested for a butty stop just after, where we ate the first six of our twelve cakes.

Yes. Twelve cakes.

No. That is not a misprint.

12. *Twelve.* T-W-E-L-V-E.

As we rounded Dornock bay, which is a very pretty bay, I have to say, we witnessed something neither of us had ever seen before: seals lying on the sandbanks lazing in the sun.

To begin with we weren't sure what we were looking at. From a distance they appeared like moving rocks and as we had not anticipated seals, we weren't thinking along those lines.

Obviously we couldn't give them a glancing look and cycle by; we had to get off the bike and drink in the scene. Their intermittent barks carried in the wind and we were spellbound with such a precious and unexpected sight.

We sang our hearts out to God as we cycled along, which is something we often did but today we did it with even more oomph.

Ian phoned shortly after and I gushed with excitement for Scotland and all things Scottish.

"I don't really like the place," he said.

He needs to do it on a bike.

He can borrow ours.

At Broro we had our second coffee and butty stop with cake numbers seven to ten from Jo. It was there we met the advance guard for a group of four who were doing LEJOG the other way round.

JOGLE, I suppose. Sounds fun, doesn't it?

Then rain set in shortly after and stayed with us the remainder of our day. Derek phoned and repeated his plan that we should do it all again.

"We'll talk about it when you get back," he said.

No chance!

If he's so blinking keen, *he* can do it!

He can borrow the bike with Ian.

Usually I hate cycling in the rain but nothing could dampen my enthusiasm today and even when Paul abandoned looking at the map and overshot our destination by more than two miles I held good.

He telephoned our host Ina and we were told to retrace our steps to a gift shop in Helmsdale where her husband Adam was working. We could leave the bike in their church hall and he would bring us by car to their home.

This we did. We squelched into his shop, squelched into his church and then squelched into his car.

Paul and I gazed at each other in fear. This man drove like a maniac, at least 50 in a 30mph zone – or so I thought until I looked surreptitiously at the speed dial.

27mph.

We had spent three weeks travelling at an average speed of 10mph and this was all wa-a-a-ay too fast.

When Ina showed us to the guest bedroom, I noticed two things straight away:

The bed was a squashed oval shape. "It's so the devil can't hide in the corners," she confided. Oka-a-ay...

And secondly, and more interestingly, there was a pile of tablet on a plate on the dressing table.

Ina had cooked a meal to feed the five thousand. We had the equivalent of a six-man steak pie each complete with seasonal veg and strawberry Pavlova.

Adam had kidney failure and Ina nursed him at home with a complete dialysis machine in their third bedroom several days a week. They both treated this imposter with humour and a combined fortitude that was both humbling and encouraging to witness.

Their dog Trigger was a sweet little thing and about as ferocious as a goldfish.

We enjoyed their company enormously and were certainly feeling quite giddy at the thought of just one day to go. To all intents and purposes we were there, and our mood was buoyant.

We both needed the inevitable toilet stop in the night and Trigger padded wearily with me as I made my way to the bathroom, nuzzling against my leg. A burglar would be in serious danger of being licked to death.

After his visit to the loo Paul climbed back into bed and asked if I'd like a little treat. I hid under the covers shaking until he produced the last two pieces of cake courtesy of Jo.

Hallelujah!

Comments / Texts

Only 2 days left, u can do it! No phone signal or wifi yesterday on Skye. Heading to Thurso 2day. Beginning to experience midges! We are looking forward to seeing you tomorrow so much. LAST DAY – ENJOY!
Love u loads.

Shirley

Arrived in Helmsdale sopping wet but happy.
Great day cycling, stunning scenery! 1 day to go!

Annie (to Super 7)

Whoop whoop!... Who cares about a little rain!!! One day!... I predict tears! Hope Shirley brings tissues!

Pam

Fantastic! It's just started chucking down here too!
All the best for tomorrow. Absorb every moment coz you won't do it again!

Helen

I can't believe that you have almost done it... Words are totally inadequate. I pray that the sun shines down on you tomorrow on the last leg of your journey, but not too hotly! Bless you both – I'm full of admiration. It has been great reading your blog each day. Thank you for sharing such a magnificent achievement with us all.

Anne

You certainly have a gift of making your trials sound hilarious. You'll look back on this with much laughter I'm sure. So close to the end now. Have you both got a week off work to recover? You are doing so well, one final push (well ok pedal) and you are finally there. I wish I could be at the finish line cheering and whooping. I am very proud of you both, a true inspiration.

Natalie

After all that sunshine and righteousness I guess you really don't mind getting sopping wet with just ONE DAY TO GO!!!! Well done. I will pass on the excitement to the Church Council tonight. Now you have to take it extra steady tomorrow taking extra care, and soaking in all that has been for the last 21 days. Prayers for safe journeying for your sister too. Love to your final hosts, blessings to all. I am just getting practice in planting 2 new Clematis for when I am up to my knees in 3 weeks of your garden growth next week!

Jude

Ian says, "Did the cakes last all day or was there a need to jettison the payload into your tummies to reduce the tare?" I say, eat as much cake as you like, you are our heroes guys!
ENJOY YOUR VERY FINAL DAY tomorrow and we can't wait to see you both returned to us safe and sound. Have a lovely final evening with your sis.

Jude

Nearly there – I can almost hear the shouts and cheers! Keep on to the end of the road.

Anne J

I seem to remember when you last preached at Wellspring that you were advertising Sue Stanmore's 'welcome home' garden event, especially with respect to the need for cakes, as you would not be able to have any on your little trip!!! Need I say more? So you'll turn up with a cake in each hand?!

Andy

I feel tired reading your wonderful blogs, I really am lost for words, it only seems a short while ago when this trip was mentioned and now you have nearly completed it... What an excuse to eat cake! I wonder what the next one will be? I think you need a quick rest before taking on another cake & coffee shop. Looking forward to catching up very soon. x
Keep on keep going. x

Rhona

Felt for you so much Annie. Wonderful you've reached the last leg and you've heard the bugles from the approaching cavalry. Pudsey bear is looking good!

Mum

3ᴿᴰ June, 2014

STAGE 20

Helmsdale to John O' Groats

"Are we nearly there yet, Paul?"

We lay in the early morning light when everything was still quiet in the house, and thought about the enormity of the day ahead. This was it. All the planning, the laughter and the tears culminated in this final day.

We pinched ourselves – and then each other, which was a lot more fun.

I commented that after all we had been through it would be jolly unfortunate if we got squished by a lorry on today of all days, and with that sobering thought we hauled ourselves out of bed for one last bike adventure.

Every day we prayed for our hosts, ourselves and for God's gracious protection and today would be no different.

Breakfast was an early affair at 7.30am as Ina had a conference to get to somewhere south of Helmsdale. Let's face it, virtually *everywhere* in Britain is somewhere south of Helmsdale.

Their church minister, John, joined us for the meal, which was a good thing as Ina had cooked a huge amount of food and Paul and I could only manage cereal. I fear she was a little disappointed with us not eating the feast spread before us but we had to cycle fifty odd miles and that's a painful process on a full stomach.

Adam took us to the church to reacquaint ourselves with the bike and I realised then I had left my cycling gloves on their radiator so had to go back to the house once more to retrieve them. Adam is a laid-back sort of person and he took it all in his stride.

We felt that Ina and Adam and Chris and Estelle, the very first couple we had met a lifetime ago in Cornwall, were like a pair of bookends at either end of the tour, and they will forever hold a special significance to us.

This was it!

John O' Groats, here we come!

We had to get out of Helsmdale first though, which proved harder than we had imagined. At breakfast we had all discussed the hills just outside the town and I quote,

"They're not too bad."

Oh, my word! Obviously our breakfast companions had never done them on a bike. The first one was pretty dire but we managed it without getting off and it was quite splendid to look back and see Helmsdale far below us; but the second one beat us to shreds and we decided to get off on a sticky looking hairpin bend and walk to the top.

Either the mist descended or we were so high we were cycling up amongst the clouds, I'm not sure, but for part of our continuing journey we couldn't see what was in front of us beyond several metres. That didn't worry me as much as the fact that any traffic behind us would have the same problem. We dressed ourselves in our bright red jackets (peas in a pod) and put our red tail light on, and I took to singing, "When I survey the wondrous cross," at the top of my voice. Every now and then I went a bit squeaky as a car dashed past, but we survived.

From here to John O' Groats the A9 follows the coast, which allowed us some spectacular sights once the mist cleared. This took my mind off the hills we had to climb.

It was a windy day so the sea was rough. There were ruinous castles dotted along the shoreline, and we passed herds of what I think were Aberdeen Angus, big woolly-looking mammoths with horns – and I am convinced to this day we saw a pair of ptarmigan.

Possibly.

Having reached the top of a certain hill, we should have stopped in traffic. The sign read, "Abnormally Wide Load," which they were waiting for to come up the other side and over the brow.

Paul clearly thought they meant me because, after seeking a quick nod of assent from the official man on duty, he just carried on cycling.

We had our twenty-mile butty stop at the side of the road and a cyclist on a Penny Farthing went past! It took us ages to catch him up; he really put a wriggle on. They look the most precarious of bikes and for the first time I thanked God I was on the back of a tandem. In a coffee shop in Wick we sat and watched him dismount and then remount a few minutes later. I can't tell you how dangerous it looked. Walking on the left side of the bike he had to place his left leg on a fixed mount about two feet off the ground and then swing his body up and over in one fluid movement, locate the saddle and start pedalling before the whole thing toppled sideways.

I checked quickly with Paul that they didn't make tandems of these contraptions. I wanted to kill any seeds in his brain before they developed into Epping Forrest.

The rider had it off to a fine art though, and we spent the rest of the journey playing leapfrog with him.

The last seventeen miles to John O' Groats were the longest of the whole tour. Shirley and Malcolm had come up to Scotland the previous week and were working their way round the west coast and over the top to meet us at JOG.

In my excitement I phoned Malcolm ten miles out to say we would be with them in an hour and then Paul chose that very moment to get his butties out and have a twenty-minute break!

I couldn't believe it. *"What are you doing?"* Oh, I was so frustrated.

He pointed out that battling the headwinds had seriously taken it out of him and he needed carbs.

We both took the opportunity to water this green and pleasant land 'au naturelle' one last time despite the landscape being quite barren without even a blade of grass to protect our modesty.

Another cyclist stopped close to us and we shared our stories. He told us he had once cycled from the UK to Australia – apart from the wet bits, obviously – and as he was speaking about what an "absolute blast" it had been, I could see the cogs in Paul's mind turning.

"Don't. Just don't," I counselled.

No matter how hard we pedalled, John O' Groats remained in the distance. The ride was painfully slow.

We had fifty-two miles to cover that day and I kept looking at the mileage counter:

47

48

48 and a half

49

49 and two feet

And so it went on.

And then out of nowhere a sign appeared:

"John O' Groats, a welcome at the end of the road."

Oh, happy, happy day!

We got off the tandem and took photos of each other there. No one else was around and we still had two miles or so to go but this was our own perfect moment. Just the two of us. We hugged and kissed tearily and then got back on the tandem to finish the business we had started three weeks ago.

John O' Groats isn't how I imagined it to be. I expected a town but it's just a series of small, individually styled hotels. It honestly looked as though a new one was built every now and then as LEJOG became more popular. We found our hotel, Seaview, easily enough but there was no sign of Shirley and Malcolm. I was disappointed and started to fret.

A hand on my shoulder and a gentle voice:

"Your sister is waiting for you down the road by the signpost."

It was Carlene, the American we had met on the road a few days earlier. I had posted her picture on our blog site and my eagle-eyed sister had recognized her, and they had spoken together.

I had forgotten all about the official signpost. If Shirley had not been there waiting for us, we probably would have got off the bike at the hotel, and that would have been that. We would have missed the opportunity of having a matching pair of signposts either end of Britain.

Once more we mounted the tandem and headed down the lane. Shirley and Malcolm saw us before we saw them, but soon I became aware of someone waving excitedly and running towards us, and at that moment I started to cry.

Even as I sit here recalling the moment I am moved to tears.

I waved back shouting and whooping with total abandon. Paul gave me the usual warning:

"Don't jump off the bike. Let me stop first or we'll topple over."

Yeah, yeah! Before he had even applied the brakes I had unclipped my feet from the pedals and was jumping off the bike. It was all he could do to keep it upright.

Shirley and I embraced. We laughed, we hugged. I said, "I don't believe we've done it," a fair few times.

Malcolm got it all on video. I hugged him too.

I went quite delirious then and hugged everyone in sight.

I hugged all the cyclists milling around, including the Penny Farthing chap, and some of the CTC group we had met near Inverness. I hugged their relatives. I hugged two women who were just about to set off from John O' Groats to Land's End on foot. I hugged the official photographer. Everyone was hugged at least once and I may have gone round again.

Just then my mobile sounded. It was Ian:

"Are you nearly there yet?"

I think he made out through the tears and excited burbling that yes, we were indeed there!

I also took the chance to phone my friend Joan who was running the Tots 'n' You group at church in my absence. They finished at 3pm, and with just ten minutes to go before they closed I rang to tell her our news so they could celebrate with us. Not that the tots, bless them, had any real idea of what we had accomplished but it was fun to hear them all shouting in the background.

At John O' Groats, if you pay, you can have an official photo taken by the signpost that can be personally adapted for you. Shirley and Malcolm afforded us this treat and the sign read,

"Paul and Annie, CRU & MRDF 1012 miles."

It should have read 1018 miles. I discovered later that we had added up wrong.

Celebrations over, we had to get back on the bike, definitely for the last time, and ride back up the lane to the hotel. It was absolutely the last 'up' of our incredible journey and I think we rode on sheer adrenalin.

Shirley had brought a proper set of clothes for each of us that I had prepared weeks ago for this most auspicious occasion, and after a shower we changed only for the second time in three weeks into something other than cycling shorts (the first time being at Bosley on day 9). Our cycling gear was consigned to plastic bags and we looked like normal people once more.

But we weren't normal.

We had done LEJOG!

Paul stretched out on the bed and read the hotel information provided. Apparently there was a woman who did LEJOG in the 1950s in just under three days. It had taken us three weeks.

Maybe they weren't so far apart back then.

We sent our final blog and then went down to the restaurant for a meal with Shirley and Malcolm. For starters Paul and I both had black pudding in sweet chilli sauce. Paul reverted to being English then and ordered steak and ale pie, while I, I tucked into haggis drizzled in a whisky sauce, which put the seal on my love affair with Scotland.

We walked along the rocks at the very tip of Britain that night and beamed like Cheshire cats whenever a camera was pointed in our direction. Back in the hotel en suite the congratulation messages began to arrive as we lay side by side in a dream.

Through reading this account of our tour you probably have come to the conclusion that Paul is a patient, gracious, positive, well-grounded character, and you would be entirely right. There is no one this side of Mars that I would ever trust with my life in the way I trust him.

You have possibly come to some conclusions about my character too. Be gentle in your assessment; I was way out of my comfort zone.

I will finish with an extract from our final blog:

"We're here, we've done it – and we are never doing it again – but *we did it!* There are 1012 miles that are forever embedded in our heads, our hearts and our bottoms. It's been a ride of a lifetime!

"We have known God's living presence with us in each day; we have witnessed stunning scenery, breathtaking beauty crafted by his hands; we have met such generous-hearted people, and been truly blessed by their hospitality; we have had good times and hard times, sometimes mile by glorious mile and sometimes inch by painful inch. In all of this we have shared our story with incredible people... *you!* You have been vital to us in your encouragement, support, prayers and (often) hilarious blogs and texts.

"Thank you!

"God bless!

"Goodnight

"Paul and Annie xx

"P.S. Does anyone want to buy a second-hand tandem?"

We couldn't sleep for excitement that night and at three in the morning I found Paul studying a map on his GPS.

"What are you doing?"

"I'm just looking at the coast-to-coast route."

Aaarrgghh!

Comments / Texts

Last day... Woohoo! Despite the huge relief and euphoria I am sure there will be a little sadness that this special time has come to an end. So incredibly proud of u both. Not many grandparents have done lejog!!!! Hope u have a fab last day. Enjoy the hotel xxxxx.

Pam

Almost there! Keep those wheels turning for one more day and yr there. U can do it! x

Jamie

Just to say we are thinking of you on your last day! You won't want to leave your final destination once you get there... or maybe you will!

Charlotte

Hi, we r birdwatching at Dunnet Head, 12 miles from JOG, what is your eta. Weather good, Keeeeep pedalling. xxxx

Malcolm

Probably about 3pm, difficult to tell, will text you when we are 10 miles away from JOG xxx. Whoopee!!!

Annie

So the big day has finally arrived. Many congratulations on your magnificent achievement.

John

Hey you'll be there today, congratulations!
Annie... did Paul not mention that
you have to cycle back?

Sally

Dear both. Just read yr blog. Very very very well done on a fantastic achievement.
Immensely proud of u! Enjoy a lie in tomorrow and the novelty of not havin to cycle! x

Jamie

Congratulations to the pair of you – that was epic! Just a thought – IF you were to cycle back then those hills that gave you such a problem getting up would be all downhill this time!?!

Sheila

We're here! We've done it! Never again!
We've done it!!

Annie (to Super 7)

Whoaaaaaaah!!!!!
CONGRATULATIONS YOU AMAZING TANDEM
TWINS. Lots and lots of love and PRAISE YOU LORD
FOR KEEPING PAUL AND ANNIE SAFE!

Jude

Woohoo!... Phone went off whilst I was teaching
lesson... Whoops!! So I told them all about u at
end! Enjoy the thought of no cycling tomorrow!

Pam

Well done, well done! Are you cycling home
tomorrow? Derek says, "Is the tandem going into
the sea at John O' Groats?" Will be nice to see you
soon. Lots of love.

Hilary

Whoop whoop!! Fantastic!! So pleased for you!!
Can't believe it's all over!! Lots of love and kisses
from all of us!! Well done!

Simon

Brilliant!! Well done!! You are mad but lovely!
Looking forward to seeing you lovely people on
Saturday. Do you think your legs are longer now
cause they have been stretched for so many days?!
David has just shouted "well done". As you are
driving from up there to down here it has to be
downhill all the way!

Catherine

STUPENDOUS!

Joan

I just wanted to burst into tears. Wonderful, the pair of you. Congratulations! All my love. Thank you for your phone call Annie. Lots of love.

Mum

Well done both of you! We are so pleased to have you as friends – boasting about you to everyone we meet. (But perhaps you had more than a little bit of help from the Lord and all those lovely people who put up with you along the way?)

Stuart and Janet

A fantastic achievement both of you. It has been great reading of your adventures every night. We too are pleased to have played a small part in this. Sleep well!

Chris and Barry

As Frazer would say in Dad's Army: "Aye, I knew you could do it all along."

Andy

Amazing! What a blessing it has been to meet you and to follow your journey. God's blessing as you come back home and settle in again and as you share your story.

Debs and Pete

Well done. What an achievement. You sure look happy in your pics. Thank you for sharing your journey with us. NOW GO REST!

Natalie

Congratulations to you both – a fantastic achievement (which wouldn't have been the case if it had all gone swimmingly...) What have you got planned for your third honeymoon?

Geoff and Claire

Very well done. We have really enjoyed your daily blogs, we will miss them!

Alec (and Ruth and Bosley friends)

AMAZING, INCREDIBLE, YOU HAVE DONE IT!!!!!
Now who do we blog to every night!
Only joking, we can talk to you now in person – much better to do that. So looking forward to seeing you guys on your return. In the meantime, enjoy your journey back with Malcolm and Shirley and take care. Lots of love and every blessing! XXXXX

Jude (and Ian)

Fantastic!

We remembered you in prayer at our house fellowship this evening and at the Congleton Bible Weekend Committee meeting this morning at the URC. Joan also told us of your safe arrival just after she had spoken with you at Tots this afternoon so as you will see you have been in our thoughts and prayers all day today. God bless you both.

It is often said after an achievement such as this, "It is something to tell the grandchildren in years to come." Happily in this case your grandchildren and family, with others, have been a great support and encouragement and have been a part of your journey for the last twenty days.

Strangers who you have never met before have become life-long friends.

It will be great to meet up again at Sue's on Saturday – lots of tea and cakes await you we are sure!! Take care and God bless, safe journey back over the border from Bonnie Scotland.

John and Margaret

Fantastic achievement!! So thrilled and delighted that you made it – very inspiring. I am really hoping that you haven't given Andy ideas about our future cycling expeditions! Have a well deserved rest and safe journey home. Lots of love to you both.

Andy and Bev

I cannot believe it is over. Just a few miles in the car now and the tandem can have a well earned rest.

Catherine

Love the photos of the two of you grinning from ear to ear… and VERY well deserved at that. Congratulations, it's an amazing feat, look forward to seeing you both VERY soon.

Rhona

You are both an inspiration – determination, filled with spirit (Holy of course), gutsy and remaining humorous… You must be v. v. proud and pleased with achievement – WELL DONE, can't say it enough!!

Geoff and Jannette

Wow, amazing! I have followed your blog all the way through. Huge well done!

Fiona

Well done Annie & Paul – amazing feat!!

Gill and Steve

Annie and Paul you are just amazing, and I think you should turn your blog into a book!! It would cheer the soul, encourage, inspire, edify and lift the readers... We need a coffee and energy bar date (I'm assuming you've given up cake now?) so you can share all the glorious and gory details!!!!!

Maz

You say you made 20 NEW sets of friends with all your hosts – does that mean Shirley & Malcolm were not your friends before?! Well done once again. Really pleased you arrived home in 'one piece' and still married!

Simon

Well my friends, your great big tea shop tour of Great Britain has sadly come to an end. Still, think of all the fun you've had; the mountains high and the valleys low. (Oh, you didn't do Wales did you? In that case it's just the mountain high then.)

Paul has been the bravest man I know cycling all that way with a smouldering Russian nuclear reactor on the back seat. I think it was a wise choice not to wear your Russian underwear in case of Chernobyl fallout. Fortunately, a full-scale meltdown was avoided and the only clatter that could be heard was that of chains falling off and hearts being set free. Amen!

This has been a great undertaking and I praise God for keeping you safe and focused. Many people are going to be helped by your hard work and devotion to God and the goal ahead. Blessings to you and thanks be to God, and also to all those people who put up with you. It wouldn't have been possible without them. Anyways up, as some queen said, "Let them eat cake," and, "Rasputin, you stink." Blessings and much praise. GOD IS GOOD ALL THE TIME AND ALL THE TIME GOD IS GOOD. xx

Ian

Chris and Estelle

Jean, David and Wendy

Matt, Anna, Malcolm, Shirley and Mum

Muriel and Mike

Debs and Pete

Dennis and Sheila

Jamie, Pam, Joseph and Daniel

John, David, Wendy and John

Bosley, Trinity and Wellspring friends

Bill and Marylyn

Julie and Ken

Hazel and Peter

Jock and Ross

May and Annie

Bruce and Sally

Chris, Annie and Barry

Mary-Ann

Alan, Shona and Buster